Treasury of
African Love

More *Treasury of Love*

Each collection also available as an Audio Book.

All prices subject to change. TO PURCHASE HIPPOCRENE
BOOKS contact your local bookstore, call (718) 454-2366, or write
to: HIPPOCRENE BOOKS, 171 Madison Avenue, New York, NY
10016. Please enclose check or money order, adding $5.00 shipping
(UPS) for the first book and $.50 for each additional book.

Treasury of African Love

Poems & Proverbs

Edited by

NICHOLAS AWDE

HIPPOCRENE BOOKS

NEW YORK

For
Anne Raufaste
&
Mark Philliskirk

ACKNOWLEDGMENTS
Gaim Kibreab, Farouque Abdillah, Christopher Shackle,
Pumla Mdotswa, Emanuela Losi, Kevin Smith, Evie Arup,
Malami Buba, Martin Orwin, Kieran Meeke, Fred Hill, Laurie
Martin, Graham Furniss (Hausa: 'Poetry Prose and Popular Culture in
Hausa'), David B. Coplan (Sesotho: 'In the Time of Cannibals'). Every
effort has been made to trace copyright holders of extracts that appear in
this book.

ISBN 0-7818-0483-3

For information, address:
HIPPOCRENE BOOKS
171 Madison Avenue • New York, NY 10016

Printed in the United States of America

Contents

Poems of Love

Proverbs of Love

Poems of Love

Baddoo qad ah iyo dhirtoo qalimmo ah
Caleenta qoyan oo qardaas laga dhigo
Haddii lagu qoro qaraamka i galay
Malaa ways qalliqi lahaayeen

If all the sea were ink, and all the trees were pens
If all the leaves so green were changed to paper thin
If thus the love which entered me were writ with all these things
Perhaps there would be just enough to write my thoughts of love for thee

—Somali Love Song

AFAR

Orowwaḥ

Bas nigaali lammam yaadige
Num numut haḍa heelam yaadige
ᶜAdgiley ᶜabalah tof ta yaadige
Bas nigaali lammam yaadige
Barayih Seger-Kibu-l hayne
Nan hereera le gaala ma naadiga
ᶜAdah idᶜa soddomul yayse
Taraadah morootomul yayse.

Yiᶜasabba daa malil ᶜale heela
Yiᶜasabba haḍ malil haḍa heela
Baruudul yaaba malaykat le
Ḥanti labha le deerol labha le
Sinlih arde linok neh idiggila
Yimaᶜabba tiktikan han le
Rukan han mali nakan han le
Baakerrik damumul radda himbo le
Bakarroyti ᶜalek radda deero le
Saᶜal kee maᶜandi waydal le
Kedok elle muddutaanam le
Yina hinna narigtiinammayii
Nargo luk narigil maydoodiney.

Yinay adheliyok yibaḍaw dihey
Waydal innah kareero meᶜaalay
Saaruh obte barul tammeekere
Tefferem mali lammam teffere
Waysi koona barih maaᶜo teffere

AFAR

Camel praise song*

So, our camels know two things:
They know the man their man fights is big like a tree
They know the naked blade dripping drops of blood
So, our camels know two things
To graze at night, we settled at Seger-Kibu
We do not know camels with narrow ridges
For beauty a herd should be of thirty
For walking in file, it should be of forty.

My dear father, in stoneless terrain she is like a hill
My dear father, in treeless terrain she is like a tree
She has speaking angels seated on her hump
She has men to milk and men to rescue her
Since we run towards you, milk her for us
My good father, she has milk we all drink at once
She has no milk to churn, but milk to sip
She has froth that falls on the lips of he who hungers
She has help from the thirsty ones of the mountains
She has the graves of men who died for her
She has what makes you superior, apart from the tribe
She is not my mother, but the she-camel's
If she has a foal, never change it for a young male.

If I call to you "My mother" – answer me "My son"
O she-camel standing proud as a warrior's tomb !
You came to Baru to graze for sweet herbs
Yet failed in nought save two things:
Five nights you could not eat in Waysu

* According to Afar convention, the she-camel here represents the poet's sweetheart.

Alsa sinni barih gedo teffere
Yoo barisse gune-h din weeh an
Yoo kee gilalak fan radey yinaay
Koo hinnay nanu ninni ma naamina
Gabbarah gulubuh geddaamak
Woomanok rabi koh yayse yinaay
Bar gedaay Badolaf-al maahisey
Lamma-Dabbi-h afal dabbaakiyey
Dayyu tin^cibek Udkooma-l daley
Gaali kihna Gabolle-l daley yinaay.

Gaalah abna ^cadab nan naadige
Abta yab nimakaaban taadige
Deero kok nimorootom duudele
Adhelem nimakaaban taadige
Deero kol gafan innah luu^cele
Masgid innah marot koo nabbide
Ummaan abba badah ma haba yinaay
Abba hela badi elle rabam me^ce
Ilmontah yenek deero beyam me^ce
An kusaaku kebel maysodoodoha
An kudro ^carik maydeleele^ca
Korte daaba wadir lilli hannito
Buufolaamo koh amballuk tene
Goobut inki mudum koh heeliyo
Rabba teh gulubul kabbaddiyo
Satto luk raatal kok araddiyo.

At night you could not walk save by moonlight
Since you taught me to eat at night I cannot sleep
Help me in the midst of the dry season, O mother !
It is not you but ourselves we mistrust
Instead of paying tribute on bended knee
Death is better for you than this harsh life, O mother !
Go by night and see the dawn at Badolaf
Stand proudly when entering Lamma-Dabba
If you desire enough water, give birth at Udkooma
Give birth, O mother at Gabolle, beloved of camels.

We know how to fight for our camels
And you know our judges' sentence in case of theft
Our forty men will stand up at your call
You know what our judges will say
And our rescue will fall on you like a cliff
Encircling you in safety like a mosque
No father abandons his child, O mother
The son who resembles his father should die there
If he is a bastard, good for him to lead the rescue party
When your day comes, I shall not change my sandals
At your call for help, I shall not stay at home
If you looked down the mountain you had climbed
Someone's oiled hair would appear to you
For you I would pierce any shield at a blow
And may I never find you hobbled and dead
For could I ever abandon your track when rescuing you !

AMHARIC

አንቺ ካልመሰለሽ

አንቺ ካልመሰለሽ
    ይቅር ምን አባቱ ፨
ለኔ አዲስ ፡ አይደለም
    ወዶ መለየቱ ፨
ከተውሽኝ ትቻለሁ
    ደህና ሁኝ እንግዲህ
አላንስም ለራሴ
    እኔም ካሁን ወዲህ ፨
ይካለኝ ለኔ
    አንቺን እምኔ ለከረምኩት ፨
ጉድ ብሏላ
    ይመጣል ብዬ ላልጠበኩት ፨
አወይ እያልኩ
    እየተገረምኩም ፨
አያዘንኩኝ
    በይ ልለይሽ መቼም ፨
አማፍቀር አልታደልኩም
    በል ልቤ
በርታ ብለህ ይህን ችግር አለፈው
    ስለ መጪው አስብ እንጂ ፨

AMHARIC

If you don't think this is proper

If you don't think this is proper
    Then hell ! let it be forgotten now
For it is no new experience for me
    To part willingly.

If you decide to abandon me here
    Then I will bid farewell to you now
Have no fear, I can take care of myself
    From now on...

I feel sad — I thought I trusted you
    But you took me unawares
This decision of yours caught me offguard
    And it has left me shocked and sad.

Yes, I must be separated from you
    For me not the gift of being loved
O my heart, give me strength to pull through
    And to face the future to come.

—*Ephrem Tamru*

ANCIENT EGYPTIAN

ANCIENT EGYPTIAN

The sickness of love

I will go home and lay me down
I will make as if I am ill
My neighbours will come to visit me
And my beloved will be there with them
Then there will be no need of physicians
Since it is she who knows what truly ails me.

I am yours

I am yours,
So where will your heart now turn ?

Would you turn away
If you seek to be fed ?
If you long to caress
My thighs and my breasts,
Be a glutton for me.

Would you turn away
If you need to be clothed ?
Surely I am clothes enough.

Would you turn away
If you hunger ?
Take my breasts,
Abundant is what they offer.

O happy is the day of your sweet embrace !

The river song

Downstream I float on the ferryboat
To the pound of the oarman's stroke,
Reeds bundled on my shoulder.
I will be soon in Ankh-Towy,
There I will tell Ptah, the Lord of Truth:
"Tonight, give me my beloved !"

Wine the river flows,
Its reeds are Ptah
Its bloom is Sekhmet
Its lotus bud is the Dew Goddess
Its lotus flower Nerfertum.

My Golden One is pure pleasure
Her beauty illuminates the land
All Memphis is a perfume bottle
Set before one so beautiful of face.

The trap

The goose cries out
Snared by my bait –
Your love snares me
And I know no means of escape.
Now I shall take up my nets
Not knowing what to tell my mother,
Since to her each day I return
When I am loaded down with catch.
But today I did not set my trap –
Today your love trapped me.

Unique is a maiden

Here begin the Words of the Great Dispenser of Entertainment . . .

Unique is a maiden, without peer
Comelier than all mankind.

Behold, she is like the Star Goddess rising
At the beginning of an auspicious year.

She is of sheen surpassing, radiant of skin
Lovely of eyes with which to gaze.

Sweet are her lips with which to speak –
She has not a word too much.

Long of neck, bright of nipples
True sapphire is her hair
Her arms surpass gold
Her fingers are like lotus flowers.

Curving buttocks, slim-waisted
Her thighs extend her perfection
Fair of gait as she treads upon the earth.

She has seized my heart with her embrace
She makes the necks of all men
Turn away dazzled at the very sight of her.

Joyous is he who embraces her
He is like the chief of all lovers.

Her going forth is seen
Just as she is – a unique maiden.

[Egyptian hieroglyphic text]

BEMBA

Mwe bankene

Mwe bankene lelo mwabwela
Mwe bankene lelo mwabwela
Mwabwelele ndo ?
Mwe bankene lelo mwabwela
Mukampa findo mukampa ne kapeyeye ?
Mukampa findo mukampa ne kapeyeye ?
Findo mukampa nebo findo mukampa ba kapeyeye ?

O my heart, do not flee !

Flees my heart swiftly
Since I remembered my love for him
You will not let me walk like other people
For you leap up from your proper place
You will not let me dress myself
Nor cover myself with my fan
Nor put antimony on my eyes
Nor perfume myself at all.
"Do not wait, but go home !"
You say to me each time I remember him
Act not for me the fool, O my heart !
Why do you act as if you are mad ?
Stay still, be calm ! My lover will come to you
But my eyes are so blinded –
Let not people say that I am
A woman who has surrendered to love.
So stand fast each time you think of him
O my heart, do not flee !

BEMBA

You who spurn me

You who spurn me, today you've returned
You who spurn me, today you've returned
Why have you returned ?
You who spurn me, today you've returned
What will you offer me now, poor soul that I am ?
What will you offer me now, poor soul that I am ?
What will you offer me now, what now, poor soul that you are ?

Nabo bakashi bangi pa menso

Nabo bakashi bangi pa menso bakashi bangi
Mfumepo kabalabila tumbi,
Mfumepo kabalabila tumbi.

Abanabo ba mama fyala pa menso ba mama fyala,
Abanabo ba mama fyala pa menso ba mama fyala.
Mfumepo kabalabila tumbi,
Mfumepo kabalabila tumbi.

Aba nabo balamu bangi pa menso balamu balamu bangi,
Aba nabo balamu bangi pa menso balamu bangi.
Mfumepo e kabalabila tumbi,
Mfumepo e kabalabila tumbi !
Mfumepo e kabalabila tumbi,
Mfumepo e kabalabila tumbi !

BERBER

Ay iṭij i d-iceṛqen

At iṭij i d-ceṛqen
Ṣṣbeḥ zik izwar s-azṛu !

Ay imjeṛṛab n lɛaceq
Melt-iyi ddwa ḥ-ḥellu.

Tin bɣiɣ ur iyi tebɣi
Tin ugiɣ la teṭṛǧu.

My wife, when I'm there . . .

My wife, when I'm there, she's my wife
But when I'm gone, that's not what she says,
But when I'm gone, that's not what she says.

My mother-in-law too, when I'm there, she's my mother-in-law,
My mother-in-law too, when I'm there, she's my mother-in-law.
But when I'm gone, that's not what she says,
But when I'm gone, that's not what she says.

My brother-in-law too, when I'm there, he's my brother, brother-in-law,
My brother-in-law too, when I'm there, he's my brother-in-law.
But when I'm gone, that's not what he says,
But when I'm gone, that's not what he says !
But when I'm gone, that's not what he says,
But when I'm gone, that's not what he says !

BERBER

Rising sun

O rising sun
Who beats on the rock in the morning !

O you who have been in love
Tell me the remedy that will help me.

For the one I want wants me not
And the one I want not awaits me.

Ass n ṛbaɛṭac si ṛemṭan

Ass n ṛbaɛṭac si Ṛemṭan
Ay selbeɣ fellam
Mi ɛaddaɣ medden zṛan-i.

Mel-iyi ṭṭaleb i m-yuran
A lqedd l-laɛlam
Armi la treggwleḍ felli.

Wekkleɣ-am kul ṣṣebyan
D at Ṛebb' anda llan
Taqciĉt ma txeddɛaḍ-iyi !

Asmi qbel ak-k-nẓeṛ

Neṭṭat: Asmi qbel ak-k-nẓeṛ
Neḍḥa-d netheyyer
Tɛuddeḍ la reggwleɣ fellak.

Yiwet lfayda d aqesseṛ
Ta nniḍnin tedher
Ay ɛammdeɣ lǧerḥ fellak.

Ziɣemma lkif-ik yexṣeṛ
Iṛuḥ deg-geɣzeṛ
Amḍiq n rrbeḥ ixḍa yak.

Neṭṭa: Asm' ay lliɣ d aɛeccasq
Tebɛaɣ timnufaq
Xedmeɣ di lḥaǧa yagi.

Crazy for you

The fourteenth day of Ramadan
I was crazy for you
They all watched as I fell under your spell.

What sorcerer can explain your magic
O girl with the figure like a lamp
That makes you flee from me so far.

I enjoin you by all the children in the world
By the men of God wherever they may be
Beautiful girl do not abandon me !

Restive horse

She: Boy, before meeting you
I was impatient
You thought I was fleeing you.

One thing was to know pleasure
And the other was clear:
For you I have accepted hurt.

But truly your spoiled pleasure
In the torrent has been swept away
Forbidden you is the way of goodness.

He: In the days when I was in love
I flirted with the rebels
For such was my life.

Ɣuṛi aɛewdiw d aṛemmaq
Si zik iḥemmaq
Ur isɛ' algam di tikli.

Mlaleɣ-d zzin aṛqaq
Ukud nemwafaq
Ihṛen uɛawdiw yessi.

Iṭij d-dehṛen di ccerq
Ssuṛa-w tendeq
Ma tellid ṭ-ṭaḥbibt dawi-yi !

Tekkat lḥenni teṭru

A taqciĉt a tameĉtuḥt
Ikkaten lḥenni teṭru.

Teṣṭenṭun deg meqyasen
Tazra n ssxab la tserru.

Yessetma timaɛzuzin
I-gewɛaṛ yiḍ amezwaru !

I had a spirited mount
Always panting
To gallop wildly.

Then I met your fine beauty
In every way agreeing with me
And my mount became restive.

At sunrise
I was black and blue
So if you truly love me then heal me !

Hard is the first night

The young girl
Applies henna between her tears.

Her bracelets jangle as she moves
Her necklace is fragrant with cloves.

Dear sisters
Hard is the first night !

COPTIC

✝ ⲀⲚⲞⲔ ⳫⳫ
 ⲀⲒⲂⲰⲔ ⲈⲞ̄ⲞⲨⲚ / ⳧Ⲛ̄ ⲞⲨⲢⲞ ⲚⲰⲚⲈ
 ⲀⲒⲈⲒ ⲈⲂⲞⲖ ⳧Ⲛ ⲞⲨ/ⲢⲞ ⲘⲠⲈⲚⲒⲠⲈ
 ⲀⲒⲂⲰⲔ ⲈⳠⲞⲨⲚ ⲚⲤⲀⲬⲰⲒ̈ /
 ⲀⲒⲈⲒ ⲈⲂⲞⲖ Ⲛ̄ⲤⲀⲢⲀⲦ
 ⲀⲒϬ︦ⲒⲚⲈ Ⲛ̄ⲤⲀⲰϥ // ⲘⲠⲀⲢⲐⲈⲚⲞⲤ
 ⲈⲨⳠⲘⲞⲞⲤ ⳧ⲒⳐ̄Ⲛ ⲞⲨ/ⲠⲨⲄⲎ Ⲙ̄ⲘⲞⲞⲨ
 ⲀⲒⲞⲨⲰⳡ ⲘⲠⲞⲨⲰⳡ /
 ⲀⲒⲠⲒⲐⲈ ⲘⲠⲞⲨⲠⲒⲐⲈ ·
 ⲀⲒⲞⲨⲰⳡ Ⲉ/ⲘⲈⲢⲈ ⲚⲒⲘ Ⲧⲱ̄ⲚⲚⲒⲘ ·
 ⲦⲞⲤ ⲆⲈ Ⲙ̄/ⲠⲈⲤⲞⲨⲰⳡ ⲈⲬⲒ̈ Ⲛ̄ⲦⲀⲠⲒ̈ ·
 ⲀⲒⲦⲞⲔⲦ ⲀⲒ̈//ⲀⳠⲈⲢⲀⲦ
 ⲀⲒⲢⲒⲘⲈ ⲀⲒⲀⳡⲀⳠⲞⲘ
 ⳡⲀⲚ/ⲦⲈ Ⲛ̄ⲢⲘⲈⲒⲞⲞⲨⲈ ⲚⲀⲂⲀⲖ
 ⳠⲰⲂⲤ Ⲛ̄ϬⲞⲠ / Ⲛ̄ⲢⲀⲦ
Ⳝ ⲎⲤⲈ Ⲣ̄ⲞⲨⲰ
Ⲭ︦Ⲉ ⲀⳠⲢⲞⲔ ⲠⲢⲰⲘⲈ / Ⲡ̄ⳡⲎⲢⲈ ⲘⲠⲢⲈ ·
 ⲈⲔⲢⲒⲘⲈ ⲈⲔⲀⳡⲀⳠⲞⲘ /
 ⳡⲀⲚⲦⲈ Ⲛ̄ⲢⲘ̄ⲈⲒⲞⲞⲨ ⲚⲈⲔⲂⲀⲖ
 ⳠⲰⲂⲤ // Ⲛ̄ϬⲞⲠ ⲚⲢⲀⲦⲔ̄ .
Ⲭ︦Ⲉ ⲚⲤⲀⲞⲨ ⲚⲤⲈ / Ⲛ̄ⲦⲈⲞⲨⲰⳡ ⲦⲀⲢⲒⲘⲈ ⲀⲚ̄ ·
 Ⲛ̄ⲦⲀⲒ̈ⲂⲰⲔ / ⲈⳠⲞⲨⲚ̄ ⳧Ⲛ ⲞⲨⲢⲱ ⲚⲰⲚⲈ ·
 ⲀⲒⲈⲒ ⲈⲂⲞⲖ / ⳧Ⲛ̄ ⲞⲨⲢⲞ Ⲙ̄ⲠⲈⲚⲒⲠⲈ ·
 ⲀⲒⲂⲰⲔ ⲈⳠⲞⲨⲚ / ⲚⲤⲀⲬⲰⲒ̈
 ⲀⲒ̈ⲈⲒ ⲈⲂⲞⲖ Ⲛ̄ⲤⲀⲢⲀⲦ
 ⲀⲒϬ︦ⲒⲚⲈ // ⲚⲤⲀⳡϥⲈ ⲘⲠⲀⲢⲐⲈⲚⲞⲤ
 ⳠⲒⳐ̄Ⲛ ⲞⲨⲠⲎⲄⲎ / Ⲙ̄ⲘⲞⲞⲨ
 ⲀⲒⲞⲨⲰⳡ ⲘⲠⲞⲨⲰ̄ⳡ
 ⲀⲒⲠⲒⲐⲈ / Ⲙ̄ⲠⲞⲨⲠⲒⲐⲈ
 ⲀⲒⲞⲨⲰⳡ ⲈⲘⲈⲢⲈ ⲚⲒⲘ / ⲦⲱⲚⲚⲒⲘ
 Ⲛ̄ⲦⲞⲤ ϬⲈ Ⲙ̄ⲠⲈⲤⲞⲨⲰⳡ ⲈⲬⲒ / Ⲛ̄ⲦⲀⲠⲒ ·

COPTIC

Love spell to Horus

☥ I am . . .* child of . . .*
I entered through a door of stone
I exited through a door of iron
I entered with my head down
I found seven maidens sitting by a spring.
I desired but they desired not,
I agreed but they agreed not.
I desired to love . . .* daughter of . . .*
But she desired not my kiss.
I strengthened myself and stood up.
I cried and sighed till the tears of my eyes
Soaked the soles of my feet.

> *Isis:* "What ails you, man, son of Re,
> Who cries and sighs till the tears of your eyes
> Soak the soles of your feet ?"

> *Horus:* "Why, Isis, do you not wish me to cry ?
> I entered through a door of stone,
> I exited through a door of iron.
> I entered with my head down,
> I exited with my feet down.
> I found seven maidens there by a spring.
> I desired but they desired not,
> I agreed but they agreed not.
> I desired to love . . .* daughter of . . .*
> But she desired not my kiss."

* Insert the relevant names of your intended here in place of the dots. This is an ancient spell based on the legend where Horus complains to his mother Isis that he has met seven maidens who have rejected his advances.

ⲭⲉⲕⲁⲃⲱⲕ ⲉⲅⲟⲩⲛ ⲉⲛ ⲟⲩⲣⲟ // ⲛⲱⲛⲉ ⲛ̄ⲥⲁⲟⲩ
ⲛ̄ⲅⲉⲓ ⲉⲃⲟⲗ ⲉⲛ̄ ⲟⲩⲣⲟ ⲙⲡⲉ/ⲛⲓⲡⲉ
ⲛ̄ϭⲓⲛⲉ ⲛ̄ⲥⲁϣϥ ⲙⲡⲁⲣⲑⲉⲛⲟⲥ /
ⲛⲅⲟⲩⲱϣ ⲛ̄ⲥⲉⲧ̄ⲙⲟⲩⲱϣ
ⲛ̄ⲅⲟⲩⲱϣ / ⲉⲙⲉⲣⲉ ⲛⲓⲙ̄ ⲧⲱⲛ̄ⲛⲓⲙ
ⲛ̄ⲧⲟⲥ ⲇⲉ ⲛⲥ/ⲧⲙⲟⲩⲱϣ ⲉⲝⲓ ⲛⲧⲉⲕⲡⲓ ·
ⲙⲡⲉⲕ//ⲧⲟⲕ ⲛ̄ⲁⲅⲉⲣⲁⲧⲕ
ⲛ̄ⲧⲉⲕ ⲥⲁϣϥ / ⲛ̄ⲗⲁⲥ ⲉⲃⲟⲗ
ⲭⲉ ⲑⲏⲧⲟⲩ̄ · Ⳅ
ⲡⲛⲟϭ ⲉⲥ̄ⲛ ⲛ̄ⲉⲡⲛⲁ̄
ⲉⲓ̄ⲟⲩⲱϣ ⲉⲧⲣⲉ / ⲛⲓⲙ̄ ⲧⲱⲛ̄ⲛⲓⲙ
ⲣ̄ⲥⲙⲉ ⲛ̄ⲥⲟⲟⲩ / ⲙⲛ̄ ⲥⲙⲉ ⲛⲟⲩϣⲏ
ⲉⲥⲁϣⲉ ⲉⲃⲟⲗ // ⲛ̄ⲥⲱⲓ
ⲛⲑⲉ ⲛ̄ⲟⲟⲩⲅⲟⲣⲉ ⲉⲁ ⲟⲩⲅⲟⲣ /
ⲛⲑⲉ ⲛⲟⲩϣⲟⲩ ⲉⲁ ⲟⲩⲕⲁⲡⲣ̄ⲥ /
ⲭⲉ ⲁⲛⲟⲕ ⲡⲉⲧⲙⲟⲩⲧⲉ
ⲛⲧⲟⲕ ⲉⲧ/[ⲭ] ⲡⲉⲟⲩⲱϣ · ·

DARI

Siṉ dàlà re koo ɲaṉa rè

Tání-ṉ rè kánjɔ́ kánjɔ́ siṉ dàlà
Siṉ dàlà re koo ɲaṉa rè
Duu a ámó yɔ ná ṉaà tè kàwɔ dií re nà.

À uu woo nán-à,
Úú wóó nán-a va
Wo rèṉ ndàà ná ì̱ rág bele
Mó ye gata-ríṉ̱.

Kíɗɔ́gɔ́ rèé vaa-nii Ngaabà
Kili vàre rèé so joo ba-pàṉ.

Isis: "Why did you enter by a door of stone
And exit by a door of iron,
And find seven maidens
And desire but they desired not,
And desire to love . . .* daughter of . . .*
But she refused your kiss ?
No, you did not strengthen yourself nor stand up,
For you sent not forth seven tongues,
Saying THETE seven times !"

O Great One among the Spirits,
I desire that . . .* daughter of . . .*
Spend forty days and forty nights
Hanging on me like a bitch for a dog,
Like a sow for a boar.
For I am the one who calls
And you are the one who must love !

DARI

Sugar cane at the field's edge

My man is slender as sugar cane –
Sugar cane at the field's edge.
The day you slay him we will both be unmarried.

Will you take a wife before me ?
Do not take a wife before me !
For if I were a mare, I'd be tied to a post
And they would come to buy me.

O beetle, the brother of Ngaba,
You, the hoe's shaft, speak the names of my parents-in-law !

Àytaḿ ji n̥íí min̥ ni dùù

Táná Àytaḿ ji n̥íí min̥ ni dùù
Góó à ni-èn̥ ji n̥íí baa ni dùù
Táná Àytaḿ ji n̥íí baa ni dùù
Bà joo re ná à vey baa ni dùù
À gùù-rà hó i̥ véy baa tí ɔŋ

Táná Màdǝ̀lénè véy baa ni dùù
Góó à ni-èn̥ i̥ véy baa ni dùù
Táná Jacquelínè véy baa ni dùù
Àytaḿ ji n̥íí min̥ ni dùù
Naá nɔɔ̀ kerí-n̥ ngán̥ i̥ ji n̥ rè.

EGYPTIAN

Inta ᶜumri

Raggaᶜuni ᶜaineik li 'ayyaam illi raaḥuu
  ᶜAllamuuni andam ᶜala al-maaḍi wi giraaḥuu
Illi shuftuh 'ablima tshuufak ᶜaineyya
  ᶜUmri daayiᶜ yaḥsibuu izaay ᶜaleyya
Inta ᶜumri illi-btida bi-nuurak ṣabaaḥuu
  'Addi ey min ᶜumri 'ablak raaḥ wa ᶜada !

Ya ḥabiibi 'addi ey min ᶜumri raaḥ
  Wa laa shaaf il-'alb 'ablak farḥa waḥda
Wa laa daa' fid-dunya gheir taᶜm il-giraaḥ
  Ibtadeyt dilwa'ti bas 'ahibbu ᶜumri
Ibtadeyt akhaaf lal-ᶜumri yigri
  Kulli farḥa ishtaqha min 'ablak khayaali

32

Aytam floats in the water of the night

Aytam's man floats in the water of the night,
My mother's fisherman floats in the river of the night,
Aytam's man floats in the river of the night.
If you won't take me, then throw yourself in the river of the night.
You've deceived me and so I fall in the river because of you.

Madeleine's man has fallen in the river of the night,
My mother's fisherman, I have fallen in the river of the night,
Jacqueline's man has fallen in the river of the night,
Aytam floats in the water of the night.
O mother of mine, see me so wretched here !

EGYPTIAN

You are my life

Your eyes took me back to days gone by
They taught me to regret the past and its wounds
All that I saw before my eyes saw you
Was a wasted life – how could they attribute it to me ?
You are my life, whose morning began with your light
How much of my life has past and gone !

O my love how much of my life has passed
Before I met you my heart saw not a single joy
And tasted nothing in this world save pain
I have only now begun to love my life
Only now have I begun to fear that my life is racing past
Every joy that I longed for before I met you was illusion

Ilta'aaha fi nuur ᶜaineik 'albi wafikri
    Yaa hayaat 'albi yaa aghla min hayaati
Liih ma 'abilniish hawaak yaa habiibi badri
    Illi shuftuh 'ablima tshuufak ᶜaineyya
ᶜUmri daayiᶜ yahsibuu izaay ᶜaleyya
    Inta ᶜumri illi-btida bi-nuurak sabaahuu.
Il-layaali'l-hilwa wash-shaw' wi'l-mahabba
    Min zamaan wa'l-'albi shaayilhum ᶜashaanak.

Du' maᶜaaya'l-hubb du' hubbuh bahibbuh
    Min hanaan 'albi illi taal shaw'u la-hanaanak
Haat ᶜaineyk tisrah fi dunyithum 'aineyya
    Haat 'iideyk tirtaah lilamsithum 'iideyya
Yaa habiibi taᶜaala wa kifaaya illi faatna
    Huwa faatna ya habiib ar-ruuh shweyya
Illi shuftuh 'ablima tshuufak ᶜaineyya
    ᶜUmri daayiᶜ yahsibuu izaay ᶜaleyya ?

Inta ᶜumri illi-btida bi-nuurak sabaahuu
    Yaa aghlaa min 'ayyami yaa 'ahlaa min 'ahlaami
Khudni li-hanaanak ᶜan il-wuguud wibᶜidni
    Baᶜiid baᶜiid 'ana winta baᶜiid baᶜiid wahdiina
Al-hubb tisha 'ayyaamna ᶜash-shaw' tinaam layaaliina
    Saalihtu bik 'ayyaami saamihtu bik az-zaman.

Nissitni bik alaami wanseet maᶜaak ash-shagan
    Raggaᶜuni ᶜaineik li 'ayyaam illi raahuu
ᶜAllamuuni andam ᶜala al-maadi wi giraahuu
    Illi shuftuh 'ablima tshuufak ᶜaineyya
ᶜUmri daayiᶜ yahsibuu izaay ᶜaleyya ?
    Inta ᶜumri illi-btida bi-nuurak sabaahuu.

My heart and mind met in the light of your eyes
O life of my heart, O more precious than my life
Why did I not encounter your love sooner
All that I saw before my eyes saw you
Was a wasted life – how could they attribute it to me ?
You are my life, whose morning began with your light
Sweet nights, passion and love
My heart has carried these for you for so long.

Taste love with me, taste its love which I love
From the tender love of my heart which has long yearned for yours
Give me your eyes, let my eyes drift off in their depths
Give me your hands, let my hands find peace in their touch
O come my love, the past is enough
It is past, O love of my soul
All that I saw before my eyes saw you
Was a wasted life – how could they attribute it to me ?

You are my life, whose morning began with your light
Oh more precious than my days, oh sweeter than my dreams
Take me to your tender love, take me far from existence
Far, far away – just you and I alone
Our days shall wake to love and our nights shall sleep to passion
Because of you I am reconciled to my life and have forgiven time.

I have forgotten my pains and my distress
Your eyes took me back to days gone by,
Taught me to regret the past and its wounds
All that I saw before my eyes saw you
Was a wasted life – how could they attribute it to me ?
You are my life, whose morning began with your light.

Waƙar Jummai

Kullum sai muna hira
A rannan ta zo hirar
Muna cikin hirarmu
Tambayar da na wa Aljuma,
"Yaya ranki ya ɓaci
Kuma na ga jikinki da sanyi ?"
Ta ce, "I Haruna
Muna cikin hirarmu
Na samu batun labari
An ce za ka Haɗejiya
Amma sai gobe da safe."
Mun yi batun ban kwananmu
Jummai ta shiga bacci.
Na dawo na kwanta
Ina ta tunanin zuci
Na a rannan ban barci ba
Ina ta tunanin Jummai.
Washegari ya waye
Na tashi nan na yi salla.
Sai na tashi na buɗe ƙofa
Sai na gano Aljuma
Da 'yar adakar makaranta
Sai na cane, "Aljuma
Gara ki je makaranta
Abin da ya dame ka
Lallai ya dame ni."
"Ko na je makarantar
Ban zan iya aikin komi ba
Na dinga tunanin zuci."
Shi kogin soyayya,

HAUSA

Jummai's* song

We were always talking
And then one day she came to chat
And as we talked
The question I asked Aljuma was,
"Why are you so sad –
And your body is so cold ?"
She said, "O Haruna,
I was chatting
And I heard that
You are going to Hadeja,
Tomorrow in the morning."
We made our farewells,
And Jummai went to her bed.
I went home and laid down,
Mulling things over in my mind,
That night I could not sleep
For thinking about Jummai.
When day dawned
I rose and said my prayers.
Then as I opened the door
I came face to face with Aljuma
Carrying her little school satchel.
So I said, "Aljuma,
You had better go to school,
What troubles you also
Troubles me deeply."
"Even if I go to school,
I won't be able to work,
I will just go on thinking."
That's the River of Love,

* 'Jummai' is the pet name for 'Aljuma.'

Ko ba ka sha ba ka ratsa.
Na tuna 'yan nan Jummai
Ai ka ji kamannun Aljuma,
Jummai ba kauri ba
Jummai ba ga tsawo ba
Ba ta ga tsawo ba
Ba ta gajarta Jummai
Jummai ba ga fara ba
Jummai ba ga baƙa ba
Idan ka gano Aljuma
Amma samalo take Jummai.
Dubi idanun Aljuma
Kamar madara nonon shanu
Ita ɗiya Aljuma
Tana tafiya Aljuma
Kun ga kamatta daban ce
Siffofinta daban ne
Ai takonta daban ne
Ko a cikin mata ma
Komai girman taro
In Jummai ba ta zo ba
Taron ba ya haske.

Tafo yaro !

Tafo yaro tafo maza !
Tafo yaro tafo maza !
Aradu bege zai kashe ni
Aradu aradu zai kashe ni !
Kadan ba ka zo ba, za ni mutuwa.

Wasa da yaro ba ni iyawa

Even if you don't drink from it, wade through it.
O I remember Jummai
And this is how she is – Aljuma:
Jummai is not fat,
Nor is she skinny.
She is not too tall,
And not too short
Jummai is not too fair,
Jummai is not too dark.
If you gaze at Aljuma
She is the picture of perfection.
Look at her eyes,
As white as cow's milk.
Aljuma is some girl –
When she goes walking,
You know she's something special,
Her looks are something special,
Her walk is something special too.
If you saw her in the company of women,
No matter how many there,
If Jummai is not present,
The gathering has no sparkle.

—*Haruna Oji*

Come young man !

Come young man, come quick !
Come young man, come quick !
By thunder, longing will destroy me
By thunder, this thunder will destroy me !
If you do not come I will surely die.

Amuse myself with a boy I can no longer

Wasa da wani ba ni iyawa
Kadan ban gan ka ba za ni shiga dawa
Kadan ba ka zo ba za ni kashe kaina
Zan shaƙe kaina da rawani.

Ba ni so ubana
Ba ni so uwata
Ban san kowa ba sai kai, mata
Kadan na gan ki da safe
Ba ni kama hankalina.

Kan ka tafi yaƙi
Da kai nake mafalki
Kan ka tafi yaƙi
Ba ni ƙamnan kowa sai kai.

Ran ban kwananmu

Na tuna ran ban kwananmu
A dandali gun wasanmu
Habibu ɗan makaranta . . .

Farin wata kal, kal, kal,
Farin wata kwana goma
Habibu mun ban kwana
Kwana bakwai ban barci ba
Ina tunanin soyayya
Habibu ɗan makaranta . . .

An ba ni tuwo, na ce a'a
An ba ni fura, na ce a'a
An ba ni ruwa, na ce a'a

Amuse myself with another I can no longer
If I cannot see you I will go off into the wilderness
If I cannot see you I will kill myself
I will hang myself with my turban.

My father I love no more
My mother I love no more
I love no one save you, as a woman
If I see you in the morning
I cannot keep hold of myself.

Before you went off to war
It was of you that I dreamt
Before you went off to war
I loved no one save you.
                              —*Uwaliya Mai Amada*

The day of our farewell

I remember the day of our farewell,
On the open space where we used to play,
Habibu, the schoolboy . . .

The moon was clear and bright,
Ten days old.
Habibu and I bade farewell to each other,
And for seven days I have not slept,
I have been thinking of love,
Habibu, the schoolboy . . .

They gave me porridge to eat and I said no,
They gave me gruel to eat and I said no,
They gave me water to drink and I said no.

Dubi jikina na rame
Nai kwatakwal duk na bushe
Ina tunani soyayya
Habibu ɗan makaranta . . .

KRIO

Mi yon yon pɔsin ?

Uspat yu de, mi yon yon pɔsin ?
Tinap, opin yu yes; yu rayt pɔsin
De kam, we kin sing ɔl kaynaba sing.
Mi fayn fayn lɔvin, yu waka dɔn dɔn.
Wɛn tu rayt pɔsin mit, waka mɔs dɔn.
Man we gɛt sɛns no se dat na tru tin.

~

Wetin na lɔv ? Lɔv nɔto nɛks wɔl tin.
Tide gladi gɛt tide yon laf.
Nɔ put at pan tin we nɔ kam yet.
Kam kis me ya, gud gud, ɛn plɛnti.
Da tin we mek yu yɔng, i nɔba kip.

—*translated by Thomas Decker*

LALA

Ne mulanda caloba

Nati ngabuke lubemba
Kalando ka akati kakoneka –
Nati ndikwe ku nsabi.

See how thin I have become,
All skin and bone and all dried up,
Thinking of love,
Habibu, the schoolboy . . .
>—*Zabiya Uwani Zakirai*

KRIO

Where are you roaming ?

O mistress mine, where are you roaming ?
O, stay and hear; your true-love's coming,
>That can sing both high and low:
Trip no further, pretty sweeting;
Journeys end in lovers meeting,
>Every wise man's son doth know.
What is love ? 'Tis not hereafter;
Present mirth hath present laughter;
>What's to come is still unsure.
In delay there lies no plenty;
Then come kiss me, sweet and twenty,
>Youth's a stuff will not endure.
>>—*from 'Twelfth Night' by William Shakespeare*

LALA

Guess I'm fooled again

I'd cross over that river
But now our bridge is burnt –
I'll fall in and be food for the fish.

Kansi mbuli tamuili kalango
Takwali bamano ?
Ne mulanda caloba.

O yerele oo !
Takwali bamano ?
Ne mulanda caloba.

MALAGASY

Tianao tahaky ny inona ange aho !

—Tianao tahaky ny inona ange aho !

—Tiako tahaky ny vary hianao.

—Tsy tianao aho azany !
Fa ataonao famonjy fo raha noana.
Tianao tahaky ny inona ange aho ?

—Tiako tahaky ny rano hianao.

—Tsy tianao aho izany !
Fa ataonao fitia momba tseroka.
Tianao tahaky ny inona ary aho ?

—Tiako tahaky ny lamba hianao.

—Tsy tianao aho izany !
Fa raha tonta afindranao
Ka tsy tsaroanao intsony.
Tianao toy ny inona ange aho ?

Girl, you're no good for me
But who's the wiser now ?
Guess I'm fooled again.

O mercy me !
Who's the wiser ?
Guess I'm fooled again.

Tell me how you love me !

—Tell me how you love me !

—I love you as I love rice.

—No, you do not love me !
You will eat me only when you are hungry.
So how do you love me ?

—I love you as I love water.

—No, you do not love me !
Your sweat will wash away your love.
So how do you love me ?

—I love you as I love my fine clothes.

—No, you do not love me !
If you fall into debt you will exchange me
And I will vanish from your memory.
So how do you love me ?

—Tiako tahaky ny tantely hianao.

—Tsy tianao aho izany !
Fa misy faikany aloanao hiany.
Tianao tahaky ny inona ange aho ?

—Tiako tahaky ny Andriamanjaka hianao.

—Tianao tokoa aho izany !

—Mandalo mahamenamaso,
Mijery mahamenatra ahy.

—Tianao tokoa aho izany !
Fa tapi-java-nirina aho,
Tapi-java-naleha.

—Tiako tahaka an'ikaky sy neny hianao.
Velona iray trano
Maty iray hazo.

Namboleko aviavy

Namboleko aviavy
Tiako hihavianao
Namboleko tanantanana
Tiako hahatana anao.

Saro-tiana toa landy mohaka hianao –
Tiana vao misaritaka
Raha lolom-pon'ny tany
Raha lolom-pon'ny lanitra.

—I love you as I love honey.

—No, you do not love me !
You leave the honeycomb when you eat.
So how do you love me ?

—I love you as I love our Prince.

—Yes, you do love me !

—His presence leaves me awestruck,
A look from him leaves me shy.

—Yes, you truly love me !
My dreams have come true,
My searching is complete.

—I love you as I love my mother and father:
Alive in one home
Laid to rest in one wood.

Fig trees I planted

Fig trees I planted
Because I wanted you to come
Palma Christi I planted
Because I wanted you in my arms.

Like delicate silk you are difficult –
The moment it is loved it tangles
So when the earth turns on you
And the sky turns on you.

Ny fahavaratra mody ririnina
Ary ny ririnina mody lohataona
Fa raha mpivady tsy mifankatia
Dia ny mpianadahy mifanaja no tsara.

Sintony hody ray saiko

Ny hanina mampanendrom-bohitra avo
Ny fitia mampamarina an-kady
Sintony hody ray saiko
Fa adala amin'ny vadin'olona.

Isika roroa tongila no misaraka

Sary miantsinanana ambony miakandrefana –
Izany hianao hono ry itsiana
Honohonoina tsy ho manina
Izaho ry itsiana tsy manin'olona afa-tsy hianao
Fa isika roroa tongila no misaraka
Raha velona koa mifandala.

Rakitsantsa

—Hay Rakitsantsa tsy nety nandro hariva
Nandro ihany ?

—Tsy hianareo re no nandroako fa ny hafa
Hazo fotsy navadiky ny rano aho

When summer turns to winter
And winter turns to spring
When husband and wife love each other not
Like brother and sister let them respect one another.

Carry me home, my heart

Desire raises you to the highest heights
Love plunges you to the lowest depths.
So carry me home, my heart
For I am mad about another's lover.

It is in our nature to part

Like east moving over west –
That is how they describe you
They say you'd have no desire
Me, I desire no one save you
Yet it is in our nature to part
Though while we live we'll love each other.

Miss Chatterbox

—Hey Miss Chatterbox, you didn't want to swim yesterday,
But today you went swimming ?

—I went swimming not for you but for others.
I am a white twig tossed on the water

Ka na hitsangana na hitsivalana
Dia tsy zehena tsy kisahina.

Fa izay tiako no alehako
No hiorika na hivalana
Na ho any Imamo na ho any Andrantsay
Kibango nandray vorona aho
Ka an-tanety tahom-boanjo tahom-boriravina
Koa raha manova ahy ka mahafoy ahy dia mba afoiko
Fa intelo izay no nisikin-kanova ka hoatra ahy ihany.

Andeha handro !

Andeha handro ! andeha handro !
Ka ery Andranonahoatra no handro
Hosory hosory ny vohoko !
Ka sambasambao ny fanosotra
Sambasamba ray voho
Tsy ho roa manana tsy ho telo manana
Fa ho ahiko izaho manosotra.

Ka raha vazo hiombonako amin'olona
Mararia sahozanin-dava
Sady tsy ho ahy no tsy ho azy.

Ary raha vazoko izaho samy irery
Aza mararay aza marikoditra
Fa mivoaka aho mivavaka matetika
Miditra aho mitsodrana madinika
Mba hahazo mitsabo anie aho ry ity !

And whether I sink or float
They'll neither mock me nor judge me.

For it's with the one I love I'll go
Be it upstream or down
Be it to Imamo or Andrantsay.
I am a ribbon bound to a bird
I am a round-leaved mountain peanut stem
And should my man leave me for another, then I'll leave him
Yet three times he's tried to change me and never found my equal.

Come swimming!

Come swimming! Come swimming!
And we will swim, there in the Water-of-Goodness
Come rub my back!
And as you rub, speak this blessing:
"O I bless you, sweet back!
May two not possess you nor three
But let you be mine alone, I who rub you.

And if I must share a lover with another
Then let her fall ill and long be weak
So she may be neither mine nor his.

And if my lover is mine only
Then let her not shiver with cold."
For when I go away, I pray often
When I return, I speak these blessings:
"O let me care for you, you before me here!"

MANDINKA

Manding muso

M be laaring fo suuto duutala
Musu koyoo ye n kuning.
A ko nye, "Nyori nga n laa."
Nga n nyaa yele, m mang feng je,
Fo kuntinyoo mung ka boyi a sanyolu kang.
N ko a ye,
"Ite mu jumaa le ti ?
Ite bota ming ?
Ite lafita mung ne la ?"
M mang m bandi nyininkaaro la
Nga a je, a be kumboo la.

A sisoo be sawungna
Ko lenjeng dongna singo.
N wulita, n siita.
N ko a ye, "Mung ne mu ?"
A ko nye, "Nte mu musoo le ti.
Fo ite mang musoo long ?"
N ko a ye, "Nte ye Manding musoo le long.
Muso meng be finding ko nte,
Muso meng nyinkeso be koyiring ko karo,
Muso meng ke i debe ko Manding basoo."

A ko nye, "Woto m baloo findi ko Manding musoo,
Kaatu fingo kanoo le ye a tinna,
N naata jang.
Kaatu fingo kanoo le ye a tinna,
N lafita n debe la.
Kaatu fingo kanoo le ye a tinna,
M be kumboo la.

MANDINKA

Mandingo woman

As I was sleeping late one night
A white woman woke me.
"Give me space," she said, "to lay me down."
I opened my eyes, and saw nothing
But her hair falling over her shoulders.
And I asked,
"Who are you ?
Where do you come from ?
What do you want ?"
I had not finished asking questions
When I saw her weeping.

Her chest was trembling
Like the legs of a dancing woman.
I arose and sat by her side,
Asking, "What is the matter ?"
Her answer came, "I am a woman.
Don't you recognize a woman ?"
And I replied, "I know only a Mandingo woman.
A woman who is black-skinned as I am,
A woman whose teeth are as white as the moon,
A woman who plaits her hair like a Mandingo mat."

She said, "Then, change my colour to a Mandingo woman's
Because it is for the love of blackness
That I came here.
Because it is for the love of blackness
That I desire to plait my hair.
It is because of my love of blackness
That I weep.

M findi ko Manding musoo,
Nga tuuro ke i ye.
M findi ko Manding musoo,
Nga taa jiyo bii i ye kolongo to ye i kuu.
M findi ko Manding musoo,
Nga lenjengo dong fo tiloo ye boyi."

Tubaabu muso ye nying ne fo n nye.
N wulita nga Ala tentu, n na fingo la.
N wulita nga Ala tentu, n na Manding dingyaa la.
N wulita nga Ala tentu, n na Afrika dingyaa la.

Kumo

A moyi, a moyi bang kumboo la,
A be kumboo la, a be kumboo la
Sewuruba tantango be kumboo la.
Kumalaa be a fo la a ye,
"Kumboo ite sewuruba tantango,
Fo m fanang si kunung-dongnaalu
Yandaa i la siino kono ning n na donkilo la."

A be kumboo la, a be kumboo la
Deenaano be siiring bulu kosoo la.
A be bulu kosoo la, a be bulu kosoo la
Deenaano be siiring a be jeloo la.
Nyimma be i dongna, a be i dongna
Musu nyimma be i dongna lenjeng juloo la.

Kumalaa be a fo la a ye,
"I dong, i dong, Nyimma, m baaring musu,
I dong, i dong, seuruba tantango dong.

Colour me like a Mandingo woman
And I shall pound for you.
Colour me like a Mandingo woman,
And I shall fetch water at the well to wash you.
Colour me like a Mandingo woman,
And I'll dance the *Lenjeng Wo* till the sun sets in the west."

That was what the white woman told me.
So I thank God that I am black.
I thank God that I am a son of Mandingo.
I thank God that I am a son of Africa.

—*Amadou Lamin Drame*

Kumo

Hear, hear it cry.
There it is crying, it is crying
The *sewuruba* drum is crying.
A crier is singing,
"Weep, you *sewuruba* drum
So that we may rock yesterday's dancers
In their sleep with our song."

There he is weeping, he is weeping
The new-born babe is sitting and clapping.
There he is clapping, he is clapping
A baby is sitting and laughing.
The beauty is dancing and dancing
A beautiful woman is dancing to the drum beat.

A crier is singing,
"Dance and dance, my beautiful sister
Dance, dance to the *sewuruba* drum beat.

Ite le mu sewuruba tantango ti,
Sewuruba tantango mu ite le ti.
Alitolu le mu Manding ti.
Manding ne mu kunung ti,
Manding ne mu bii ti,
Mandiong ne mu saama ti."

MAASAI

Irrepeta esiankiki

Etukusho olmuruo tiauluo
Neyau enkushoto oltiren
Akiti enkushoto olpayian lai
Mirra ilmoru le nkima
Amu iyie otiaaka oloo Namerae
Ino irraga enkaji e mampai
Neme enkerai nang'arie kina
Neme enaikau pantawuo
Niyiolo kibirot inkabur
Meiba nkiri tenetumo.

Lopayian irragie matata
Mairoto sirkon pee kipuo
Airoto nempirdai ashipa
Naitoki airot Noolmong'i
Ayiolo ajo oloika ade alo
Namanya emarti enkurrarru
Namanyaenkurrarru Ole Kaigil
Laashomie nkiri bata
Elong'o sampu oo Mosomba
Naiuso Ilkokoyo le Nteyia.

You are the Mandingo drum beat,
The Mandingo drum beat is you.
You are Mandingo.
Mandingo is the past,
Mandingo is the present,
Mandingo is the future."

—*Amadou Lamin Drame*

MAASAI

Song of a woman

Rage fell upon a man outside our village
And he has brought it back with him
Yet be still, O my husband
And shatter not our hearthstones
For it was you who told Namarae's brother
To visit that young woman's house –
But as a child I never shared a breast with him
Nor is he my co-wife's first born
And we all know the flesh of youth's bloom
Is not averse to joining together.

So lay down your fury old man
Let us load the donkeys and move on –
Nempirdai I have loaded with good cheer
And Noolmong'i too I have laden
Knowing that I am bound for the highlands
Where dwells He-of-the-Ostrich-Feather headdress
Where dwells the headdress of Ole Kaigal
And where my own self felt no safety –
That mottled spear, brother of Mosomba
Who laid so waste the Kikuyu of Ndeyia.

Irrepeta e Mopoi

Kaji kirrepieki Ololtibili
Meishoru enkolong' olpurkel
Mikirrepi te saa sita
Nailirie oladalu nkishu
Nimikirrepi etadoyie enkolong'
Meya irrepeta oldalati
Enkolong' ake nalotu ene wueji
Nerrepi oloduru ng'amaro.

Eitu ashurtaki entilata ino
Olalaa ooki naishi
Atanapa enyorrata olchore lai
Ebaiki apa ara enkiti kerai
Atanapa entilata tolodua
Metubulu anaa nkolong'i.

Mapik enyorrata olchore lai
Elukunya natii ilbeli
Etirisha ilkimojik ondapi
Nerish entanun o emoinyua
Nedoyio enyorrata olchore lai
Alo eneirragie ng'aturan
Enenapieki nkera akke apik
Metubulu anaa nkolong'i.

Oltung'ani oiba nayor ilmurran
Ng'oru nabo ngol nias
Tikirrie obaribara iltuli
Meshomo aipang' te Nairobi
Tipika emuata olng'ojine
Nipik olowuaru ronkai
Ore pee ekenyua eserian intare

Mopoi's Love Song

When can I sing your praises, O Ololtibili ?
Not now in the furnace of summer heat –
I cannot sing them in the noonday sun
For then its rays make the cows listless
But nor can I sing them in the setting sun
For with its light it will take my praises
No – only after the last ray is extinguished
Will I sing your praises, my Scarlet One.

Such feelings as you awoke in me
I never spoke of them at the well
This love of you, my love, I have kept
Within me ever since I was a girl –
In the depth of my gall bladder I stored it
And nurtured it day by day.

I dare not keep this precious love of my love
In my brain, for the mind forever changes
No – it glows between my palms and fingers
Between my spleen and my liver too
Indeed, the love of my love has flowed
Down to where the infants lie
And where infants are borne I bear it
To keep it from growing day after day.

O you, so jealous of my love for my warrior
Set yourself the hardest of tasks to fulfil –
Drag yourself by the buttocks on the stoniest road
Until you have travelled to far off Nairobi
There find a hyena and put it in a sheep pen
Put there too the slim beast – the cheetah
And if by daybreak the sheep still live

Napal Ole ng'oto Talash
Tang'orokoki oloibor kume
Maitashalunyie loolpapit.

MBOSI

Ngɔndɔ

La yaa osia
Mbi mwandza o kari ibia.

Bvundu ba imbɔndɔ
Mbi atsombo ba otura.

Ɔkiɛsi dzunhu-dzunhu
Mbi atsombo a koyi kɔ.

Lea nɔ boso
Nga i sɔngɔ nɔ osina.

Imbɔndɔ ma otsinga
Imbɔndɔ mbi ikieni ba okwele
Elenge la otiri
Mbi okonda ma osia.

Panyaa abɛɛ abaa
Mbi oponga ma akanya
Inɔɔ ma abɛɛ mi tiraa
Mbi o bɔyi mbvua.

Akingi ma apfuru
Mbi mbɔmɔ a dingi osemba

Then will I abandon the brother of Talash
Then may you bleed the white-nosed donkey
To purge me of my sweet long-haired love.

MBOSI

The Beauty

She appeared in the distance, tall
As the lightning that brushes a high palm tree.

The soft noise of her supple legs
Is like the compact stir of boars bursting out.

The warm hue of her skin
Is like a nightowl's plumage eager to enter the forest.

Come, draw near !
That I may contemplate your figure.

Your legs so well formed –
Your legs trace the slenderness of the *okwele* tree,
Your face is calm and clear
Like the line of the horizon of a far-off forest.

The small space that separates your two breasts
Is beautiful like the wake of the *akanya* fish's fin,
The tips of your breasts shiver
As if you were soaked by the rain !

Your neck curves beautifully
Like a boa powerfully coiling high up an anthill,

Kingi mbi epfwa ngongo
Kingi ikiɛli ikiɛli
Mbi ɔkiɛli ma ibia.

Misi mbi akiɛ a nyɔmbɔ
Misi mbi akiɛ ma andzundza.

Mina sa ɔnɔɔ
Mbi itsɛnyii a pfulu
Mbalamwɛ mbi epaa okanda.

A di bɔ mo obee
Mbi ɔtɛrɛ mo ɔtsɛ
Ndzoro ba wɔmbɔ.

Bisi na lɔ !

Bisi la nɔ ngo
Bisi la wa
Ma e e e !
Bisi la nɔ ngo
Bisi la nɔ
Obvu bo sia nɔ oyaa ?
Mwana bare !
O taa abangi ma apɛrɛ
Onyama a ndzɔyi ma ikomba

Nga li dwa nɔ la nda ?
Nga li dwa nɔ la bare ma akoo
Nga li dwa nɔ la bola bo okiena
Akoo ma phemba mo opnga
Nga li dwa nɔ la nda ?

Your neck is a young gazelle's,
The folds of your neck
Are like the smooth trunk of a palm tree !

Your sleepy eyes are small like lamprey eggs,
Your eyes are white, big and small, like eggs of the *ndzundza* bird.

Your teeth are pretty and small
Like stalks of straw,
Your belly is supple and smooth like a tender stem of asparagus.

And there she reclines on the bed,
Compact like a willow basket filled with salt,
Her body so perfect she floats in the air !

Us two !

Us two, poor us !
You and I
Alas !
Us two, poor us
Us two, truly
In what season will you return ?
O child of others !
Take care of yourself ! Lies are all around you
A baby elephant is carried on one's shoulders,
                                   so precious it is
Who will I ask for news of you ? –
To those who go and come on the roads ?
To you, O youngest sister ? –
My feet walk tirelessly on the highway
Who will I ask for news of you ?

Uuu uuu uuu !
Nga li dwa nɔ la nda ?
Obia okambi
Mwana bare
Bisi la wa.

Yaa arfaasaa ganna

Yaa karaxiitii jirbii
    Yaa abaaboo daraar !
Yaa arfaasaa gannaa
    Yaa abaaboo !
Ati assiqii sirbii
    Yaa abaaboo !
Yaa kalaamee shagga
    Yaa abaaboo !
Nu samaanaa qabnaa
    Yaa abaaboo !
Akk'arfasaa gannaa . . .

Letebele la nka moea oaka

Ke ratile ngoanana oa Mothepu;
Letebele la nka moea oaka:
Le fofa ka ona hara litoropo
Hara litsotsi, hara malaeta.

O woe is me !
Who will I ask for news of you ?
My love
O child of others
You and I, heart to heart.

OROMO

O autumn of the rains

O bag full of cotton
    O flower flourish !
Oh autumn of the rains
    O flower !
Come near me and dance
    O flower !
O slender one, O beautiful one
    O flower !
Let us join like the first rains
    O flower !
And like the autumn of the rains . . .

SESOTHO

A Xhosa has taken my love

I love a child of the Thembu;
A Xhosa has taken my love:
She flies about with it in towns
Among gangsters, among thugs.

Le matha ka thipa;
Ke matha ka thipa libeseng mona,
Ke sena le soka ea ho palama bese:
Lampisi o batla batho lipasa;
Liphomene li batloa ke Matatane –
Oa tseba, le teng ke qhala
      le joala lekeicheng.

Bakhototsi

Hele helele ngoana moshanyana !
Ke lahlehetsoe ke motho tsamaeong;
Jo, 'Malebenyaeeeeeee !
Hae oele oelele le le oele !

Menejara komponeng koana, bo !
Ke re, 'menejara komponeng koana,
U romme manekapotene komponeng.
Heena uena, ngoana moshanyana !

'Maene kapotene, Satane,
Jo ! O moleko oa ho qetela.
Hele helele, ngoana moshanyana !

U nkile themba la ka;
O le behile merafong koana.
Hela uenaeeeee !
Ke eane, u chofa likolofane,
Mose hara makhooa koana.

I run about with a knife;
I run about with a knife in buses,
Without even sixpence for the fare:
The inspector wants people's tickets;
The cheats are wanted by Matatane –
Remember then how I spilt my beer all
      over the place in my drunkenness.

—*Majara Majara*

The thieves

Hey there man-child !
I've been abandoned by my man amid my wanderings;
Jo, 'Malebenyaeeeeeee !
Hae oele oelele le le oele !

The manager of yonder compound, *bo !*
I say, the manager of yonder compound,
You see the compound captains on your business.
Hey man-child !

Mine captain, Satan,
Jo ! You are misfortune itself.
Hey there, man-child !

You have taken my one hope;
You have kept him at the mines yonder.
Hey you, heyyy !
There he is, pushing ore-buckets,
There among the white men yonder.

—*Thakane Mahlasi*

SHONA

Rudo rwedu pedyo nerwizi

Zuva rechando rinotapira rave pakati penzira yaro,
Makura ose eve machena mashanga awo apfukudzika,
Mwoyo wako nomwoyo wangu yakasangana inorufaro,
Ikarangana kufambafamba pedyo nerwizi rwemvura zhinji.

Tiri vaviri, mudiwa wangu, takasimuka paimba yedu
Takatangisa karwendo kedu tine rufaro rwakarurama;
Pedyo nepedyo takasungana mumwoyo yedu norudo rwedu,
Tikasangana navanhu vaye vanorukudzo runoshamisa.

Nomurusango takapfunra tikayambuka notukoronga
Twusine mvura twakangooma munyika iye yeshapa chena
Tichitaura zvinyoronyoro dakara rwizi rwemihoronga
Inobereka pamunhuruka mvura yonaya vanhu vorima.

Pedyo nerwizi, padziva guru rakati svii nemvura zhinji,
Rinoyambukwa neigwa guru nguva yezhizha mvura yawanda,
Rine mitepe inoyevedza mhiri nemhiri netsanga zhinji,
Takazorora tiri vaviri tigere pasi pedyo nepedyo.

Takataura zvinyoronyoro nemazwi edu anotapira
Munzeve dzedu, tichionana uso nouso hunonyemwerera
Norudo rwedu runoerera mukati medu rwofashukira,
Rwangu kwauri, rwako kwandiri, tosanganiswa mukati marwo.

Panzvimbo yose takave toga kure nevanhu veguta redu,
Tichiyevedzwa nemvura zhinji inoerera zvinyoronyoro
Inofanana norudo rwedu runoerera mukati medu;
Nezvinhu zvose zvataiona zvakatikomba – mabwe nemiti.

SHONA

Our love by the river

Moontime, sun yellows down –
There the field, stubbled, bare,
We two together, sharing joy,
Walking, smiling-eyed, to the rushing river.

Leaving our home behind us
Sauntering, no rush, full of each other –
Close, we touch and touch, love kindled,
Passing us, our people, gently greeting.

Through the gaunt woods, across the drift hills,
We murmur softly – nearing the
Mhanyami river, now violent,
Rushing water lined with *horonga* willows.

Hitting the wet bank, looking down into pools so deep
There, where big boats ferry in summer,
Now, sweet-swaying willows, hanging
Over the foaming banks of reeds.

Talking, we talk, the words are sweet,
Our ears full of their honey, our eyes
Filling our faces, all love, and the water outside,
Inside all calm love, you and me, the easy cross-over.

In every place we are alone, but we want more,
So we walk on, following the coursing waters,
Our own currents cutting the channels deeper,
Our own moss and rocks and trees our inner landscape.

Nechinguvana, takasimuka tokwira narwo rwizi rukuru,
Tichipesana nemvura zhinji inoerera kumavirira.
Zvinyoronyoro, nepamatombo akatyandara makurukuru,
Takadevana naye Mhanyami rwizi rukuru rwenyika yedu.

Panguva yose takataura nyaya dzorudo nedzorufaro,
Tichiyeuka misi yakare yokutangisa kworudo rwedu
Yataidisa noknutsvaka musi wanhasi unorufaro
Watinogara tiri vaviri murudo rwedu rwnsingapere.

Zuva rogara makomo aye makurokuru emavirira
Njiva nedzimwe shiri dzesango dzonanga dzose kuruzororo,
Takarusiya rwizi rukuru tine rugfaro nokuwirira
Munzira yedu yaititora kuguta redu rorunyararo.

Mazuva ose, mudiwa wangu, ndinorufunga rufaro rwedu,
Norudo rwedu pedyo nerwizi runoerera zvinyoronyoro;
Hazvichadzima kunyange rinhi, zvichasaruka mumwoyo yedu,
Tichazvifunga misi nemisi dakara zuva ratinoguma.

SOMALI

Dayaxa nuurkiisa oon dib u iftiiminow

Dalkeenniyo Reer Caloo deyr la kala marshow

Cirkoo di'i waayay oo dunidu ciirtayow

Dayaxa nuurkiisa oon dib u iftiiminow
Shamsada oo daalacdoo laga dam siiyayow
Basra timirtii ka imanaysay oo baddii xidhdhow

Then, so secure, handholding, watching the outer ſtream,
Our eyes tugged by the rush and push,
We search out, then gingerly ſtep on the flat ſtones
Moving over the white spray of the mighty Mhanyami.

All the while we recalled our firſt days of love,
Calling back the ſtreams of flowing love,
Floating ſtill on the water's back with love,
Conjuring up the future of love, joined forever.

Sun was no friend, now eating the treetops
Doves and water birds seek the thick boughs for reſt
Warned by the flutter, dimness on river, peacefully
We turn homewards, leaving the water for our own neſt.

So, each day, my beloved, our shared love lives,
And our happy days on the river's edge flows in our hearts
These moments permanent in our memory, engraved in our breaſts
Breathe like eternal flowers, spring and summer till our laſt fall.

—*Luke C. Chidavaenzi*

SOMALI

Lament for a dead lover

You were the fence ſtanding between our land and
     the descendants of Ali
Now in your departure you are the sky which gives
     no rain while miſt shrouds the world
The moon that shines no more
The risen sun extinguished
The dates on their way from Basra cut off by the seas.

—*Siraad Xaad*

Miyaan masaalkaa helayaa ?

Subeeciyad wiil benderi baadhasho u tegow
Kaatun feyruusi oo kuman la siiyayow
Miyaan masaalkaa helayaa, mar la i tusyow ?
Dallaayadii waa jabtaa, biraha duubanow
Dahabka Nayroobi oo daacad loo tumow
Shamsada oo soo baxdiyo shaaca waaberow
Miyaan masaalkaa helayaa, mar la i tusyow ?

Kii dhab ah jacaylkuna

Dhirta xididka hoosaa,
Dhulka loogu beer e,
Way dhici lahaayeen e,
Dhismahooda weeyee,
Kii dhab ah jacaylkuna,
Kii dhab ah jacaylkuna,
Halkii kama dhaqaaqoo,
Dhidib baa u aasan e.

Sida dhumucda weeyaan,
Jirridda iyo dhuuxa e,
Dhererkiyo laxaadkana,
Waa Laysku dhaabee,
Kii dhab ah jacaylkuna,
Kii dhab ah jacaylkuna,
Lama kala dhantaaloo,
Lafuhuu dhammeeyaa.

Sida dhudaha weeyaan,
Isu dheellitiraanoo,

Will I ever find your like ?

You are the kilt a young dandy set out to choose
You are the fine ring for which thousands were paid
Will I ever find your like, you who have been shown to me but once ?
An umbrella that unfolds, yet you are as strong as looped iron
You who are as the gold of Nairobi, finely molded
You are the risen sun, and the early rays of dawn
Will I ever find your like, you who have been shown to me only once ?

Love that is is true

Trees are planted in the earth
So their roots are set below
If not they would surely fall
Such is the way they are
– And love that is true
Love that is is true
Shall never move from its place
For its centre is rooted firm in the ground.

Love is like the thickness
Of a treetrunk and its sap
Such loftiness and resilience
Are intertwined there
– And love that is true
Love that is is true
Shall never be split asunder
For it reaches right to the core.

Love is like a copse of willowy trees
That balance each other true

Mid ba dhan u baxaysee,
Dhinaca isa saaree,
Kii dhab ah jacaylkuna,
Kii dhab ah jacaylkuna,
Waa dhaqan wadaagiyo,
Isu dhalasho daacad ah.

Sida dhalanka weeyaan,
Dheehaa caleentu ye,
Ubax wada dhalaaliyo,
Dhimbiishaa hadhaysee,
Kii dhab ah jacaylkuna,
Kii dhab ah jacaylkuna,
Waa dhool hillaac iyo,
Dhibic-roob ku haysee.

Waa sida dhillowyahan,
Intuu laan iskaga dhegey,
Dhexda loogu marayoo
Dhakhso uga baxaayee,
Kol hadduu dhab naga yahay,
Kala dhuuman maaynoo,
Kala dhuuman maaynoo,
Waagaa dharaar noqon.

SWAHILI

Amina

Amina umejitenga
Kama ua umefunga
Nakuombea mwanga
Mapenzi tuliyofunga

kufa umetangulia
baada ya kuchanua
peponi kukubaliwa
hapana wa kufungua.

Each branch grows straight
Embracing the others by its side
– And love that is true
Love that is is true
Shall always share life's ways
Born faithful to each other.

Love is like the green grass
The shade of all the leaves
The colour of all the flowers
The hue of all the seeds
– And love that is true
Love that is is true
Is thunder and lightning
The rainclouds and their drops.

Love is like mistletoe
After it has encircled a branch
And entwined itself its length
Growing swiftly ever upward
– Once love is true for us
We cannot hide from one another
We can never hide from one another –
And then our dawn will turn to day.

—*Xusayn Aw Faarax*

SWAHILI

Amina

Amina, now you've departed, the first of us to pass
Like a flower after its first blossom you closed
I pray, my light, that you are in Heaven's welcome
For the love that we shared will never be extinguished.

Nilitaka unyanyuke   kwa kukuombea dua
Sikupenda ushindike   maradhi kukuchukua
Ila kwa rehema yake   Mungu amekuchagua
Mapenzi tuliyofunga   hapana wa kufungua.

Majonzi hayaneneki   kila nikikumbukia
Nawaza kile na hiki   naona kama ruia
Mauti siyasadiki   kuwa mwisho wa dunia
Mapenzi tuliyofunga   hapana wa kufungua.

Nasadiki haziozi   roho hazitapotea
Twafuata wokezi   kwa mauti kutujia
Nawe wangu mpenzi   Peponi utaingia
Mapenzi tuliyofunga   hapana wa kufungua.

Jambo moja nakumbuka   sahihi ninalijua
Kuwa sasa umefika   ta'bu isikosumbua
Kwayo nimefurahika   nyuma nilikobakia
Mapenzi tuliyofunga   hapana wa kufungua.

Ninamaliza kutunga   kwa kukuombea dua
Vumbi tena likunga   roho likirudishiwa
Mauti yakijitenga   mapenzi yatarejea
Mapenzi tuliyofunga   hapana wa kufungua.

Oa !

Oa	sioe anzali	mwenye mwenendo mbovu
Oa	sioe jamali	wa akili tepetevu
Oa	sioe jahili	jitu lenye ushupavu
Oa	muovu sioe	oa mwana kwetu oa !

I longed for your return, every prayer for you alone
Your defeat I never wanted, nor your departure in illness
And through His loving mercy, you came to be God's choice
But the love that we shared will never be extinguished.

No words describe my sorrow, not a second is forgotten
Forever in my thoughts, yet so distant it seems a dream
Death I never believed – life's ending and all that exists
Yet the love that we shared will never be extinguished.

That souls perish I do not believe nor they are lost forever
On the road to salvation we tread, we all meet death's angel
My loved companion, you have passed Heaven's gates
And the love that we shared will never be extinguished.

Yet a thought comes to me of which I am most certain
It is this, that now you are free from pain and suffering
Such knowledge gives me comfort, abandoned here as I am
For the love that we shared will never be extinguished.

No more ! I cannot write another word, but still I pray for you
Scattered dust reunites as the soul joins it once more
And with death's receding force, so our love shall return –
The love we shared, the love that will never be extinguished.

—Shaaban Robert

Marry !

Marry	don't marry an outcast	whose looks lack manners
Marry	don't marry the beauty	scattered in her thoughts
Marry	don't marry the pagan	overproud and vulgar
Marry	don't marry waywardness	marry one who has our ways !

Oa	akupendezaye	kwa umbile na tabia
Oa	binti ya babaye	mtambuzi wa sheria
Oa	mwali ajuaye	vyuoni aloingia
Oa	muovu sioe	oa mwana kwetu oa !

Oa	mke kufu yako	mnayefanana hali
Oa	wa kikozi chako	wa asili na fasili
Oa	binti ami yako	ikuwiyapo sahali
Oa	muovu sioe	oa mwana kwetu oa !

Oa	mrembo wa shani	mwenye hadhi na murua
Oa	mwema na watani	uwezapo mgundua
Oa	sioe muhuni	moto umejipalia
Oa	muovu sioe	oa mwana kwetu oa !

Oa	mtendee wema	mkeo uliye naye
Oa	uwe wa huruma	roho yake ituliye
Oa	mjaze heshima	japo akuzuzukiye
Oa	muovu sio	oa mwana kwetu oa !

Oa	wa macho laini	yaengayo majimaji
Oa	kwenda yu amini moyo	akakufariji
Oa	khasa mwana ndani	asojua upitaji
Oa	muovu sioe	oa mwana kwetu oa !

Oa	nakwiambia oa	jaribu tena na tena
Oa	kwa kuangalia	na kumuomba Rabana
Oa	upate tulia	na kuepuka fitina
Oa	muovu sioe	oa mwana kwetu oa !

Oa	imebadilika	dunia yenda kinyume
Oa	hutaazirika	ukiwa mbora mume
Oa	ninavyoandika	nitamkayo yapime
Oa	muovu sioe	oa mwana kwetu oa !

Marry	she who takes your fancy	beauty in body and soul
Marry	the legitimate child	knowledgeable of God's law
Marry	the initiated maiden	wise to the ways of womanhood
Marry	don't marry waywardness	marry one who has our ways !

Marry	she of the same roots	your mirror image indeed
Marry	one of your rank	of equal blood and breeding
Marry	your uncle's daughter	if perchance it happen
Marry	don't marry waywardness	marry one who has our ways !

Marry	the beauty of beauties	with aura pure and elegance
Marry	a good and civil woman	if you find yourself with one
Marry	don't marry an extrovert	a fire whose blaze you fan
Marry	don't marry waywardness	marry one who has our ways !

Marry	treat her best of all	the wife you come to choose
Marry	be ever compassionate	she should be always at her ease
Marry	and give her respect	even she who is flirtatious
Marry	don't marry waywardness	marry one who has our ways !

Marry	she who has soft eyes	which glisten and sparkle
Marry	where your heart trusts	she who will enrich you
Marry	yes, she without blemish	innocent and untouched
Marry	don't marry waywardness	marry one who has our ways !

Marry	I tell you marry !	try and try again
Marry	and do so with care	pray for her to Our Lord
Marry	seek to settle down	don't court wagging tongues
Marry	don't marry waywardness	marry one who has our ways !

Marry	everything changes	the world is spinning backwards
Marry	never feel ashamed	but be a better husband
Marry	the way I write it down	think of what I say
Marry	don't marry waywardness	marry one who has our ways !

Oa	ninakhitimia	mwema ana mwisho mwema
Oa	muovu tambua	hadi yake ni kuzama
Oa	nakariri oa	kuoa kuna salama
Oa	muovu sioe	oa mwana kwetu oa !

Mazoea yana tabu

Mazoea yana tabu
Tabia zikilingana
Tena ni kubwa adhabu
Watu nyinyi kuachana.
Hamuioni sababu
maovu kutendeana.

Usiku kucha silali
Nikaapo hukuona
Zinaniruka akili
Hukitwa kwa lako jina
Kumbe ni chako kivuli
Mwenyewe sinawe tena.

Nyama zetu za ulimi
Ambazo tukipeana.
Na mengineyo sisemi
Mengi tukifanyiana
Ni mageni kwangu mimi
Sijapata kuyaona.

Mithali watoto pacha
Jinsi tulivyofanana.
Mpenzi umeniwacha
Uhai sinao tena.

Marry	now I put a seal on this	a good person brings a good end
Marry	beware a bad person	whose end is always drowning
Marry	I command you, marry !	for marriage brings you peace
Marry	don't marry waywardness	marry one who has our ways !

—*Kaluta Amri Abedi*

What once we had . . .

What once we had is now a trial
Our souls had fused together
But now it is such torture –
See what torture – to part.
Can you ever see why
We do one another harm.

All night long I toss and turn
Unable to sit for visions of you
Slowly going out of my mind
I call out to you by name
But no – it's only your shadow
And you are no longer mine alone.

The heat of our tongues
Which we so exchanged –
I cannot say another word !
Nor of all that we did together
Such things of wonder now
The like I've not seen since.

Like twins inseparable
We moved as one body –
O my love now you've left me
And now I've lost my life

Nateseka kutwa kucha
Dawa yangu kukuona.

Tini tunda la tamasha

Tini tunda la tamasha
Mgeni kukirimiwa
Tena linapumbazisha
Akili hukupunguwa
Kwa mtu aso bashasha
Thamani akalitowa.

Iko mbali ladha yake
Ina tabu kuijuwa
Kishindo ni sumu yake
Wahali wa kuchafuwa
Huipati raha yake
Illa kwa moyo kutuwa.

Enyi walaji wa tini
Ambao munaijuwa
Kama sivyo nisuteni
Msiniache kuzuwa.
Wallahi hulili tini
Kama si mtu mwelewa.

Kwa rahisi hulipati
Si tunda la kupomowa
Huanguka kwa sauti
Na maneno yamuvuwa.
Sura yake tafauti
Na hadhi iliyopewa.

From dawn to dusk I suffer
The sight of you my only cure.

The fig is the fruit of love

The fig is the fruit of love
To bestow upon a guest
It brings with it comfort too
And sets your cares to rest
But not for those who know not pleasure
For they shall debase it.

Distant is its sweetness
Difficult is its taste
It can make problems that poison it
Create a situation that spoils
And you shall gain no pleasure from it
Unless your mind is at ease.

O you who have tasted the fig
O you who have enjoyed it
Tell me if I speak untruth
Permit me not to lie
By God you shall not enjoy the fig
If you understand it not.

It shall not come to you easily
It is a fruit not easily shaken down
It may fall with the greatest crash
And its words will undress you
Then its shape may be quite different
From the good luck it was given.

Wagombanao hupatana

Wagombao hupatana
Na tupatane mpenzi.
Mpenzi furaha sina.
Sijimudu sijiwezi
Natamani kukuona
Na isifikie mwezi.

Pumzi zimenipaa
Hazipandi hazishuki.
Majonzi yamenijaa.
Mpenzi wangu sadiki
Kuishi sina tamaa
Iwapo hunasihiki.

Mpenzi ninakuishi
Sahau yaliyopita
Nionayo sifurahi
Na swaha zikinikata.
Nakuapia wallahi
Ninakutaka widdata.

Adhabu nimeyoridhi
Upendavyo niadhibu.
Ukinipiga ni radhi
Vyo vyote sitokujibu
Maadamu nimekuudhi
Kunirudi ni wajibu.

Pendo ninakushitaki
Mpenzi waniadhibu
Ufanyayo siyo haki
Kunipatisha aibu.

Quarrellers can be reconciled

Quarrellers can be reconciled
So let us be reconciled, my love
For joy has left me, my love
And I can do nothing now
But to see you is all I desire
And a month is far too long.

My breast is all aflutter
I am left breathless
I am full of sadness
My love, believe me
To live has no meaning
If I cannot convince you.

I beg you, my love
To forget the past
All joy has left my heart
I am wracked with pain
As God is my witness
I want you and need you.

However you see fit to punish me
I will accept your choice
If you were to beat me
I would not object
The fault is mine for vexing you
Thus you should punish me.

Love you stand accused
My loved one is my tormentor
I am so filled with shame
For the wrong that you do me

Wanichimbia handaki
Mimi wako nalitubu.

Shamsa

Mwenye uso wa shamsa
Mwenye nuru ya daima
Mwenye umbo la anasa
Ndotoni nimekutuma
Pale ulipopapasa.
Rudi tena akirama.

Mbele zangu umetusa
Ewe mwenye takirima
Huzikumbuka anisa
Usiku na nuru njema
Pale ulipopapasa
Rudi tena akirama.

Sishi kichwa kutikisa
Nakutua nyonda kwima.
Jana huona ni sasa.
Moyoni umekiyama.
Pale ulipopapasa
Rudi tena akirama.

Nakuombea shamsa
Fuadi na kulla njema
Fahamu ukinitesa
Nitateseka daima
Pale ulipopapasa
Rudi tena akirama.

The hole you dig is for me
In contrition I offer myself to you.

Sunshine

Yours is the face of the sun
Light everlasting
Yours is the shape of joy
I dreamt you sent your hand back
There where you caressed me
O come again my dearest.

You have avoided me
You noble one
I have memories of joy
Your sunshine in the night
There where you caressed me
O come again my dearest.

I never stop shaking my head
Trying my sweet to hush you
To me yesterday feels like today
And in my heart you have risen
There where you caressed me
O come again my dearest.

Sunshine of mine to you I pray
A heart and all things good
I am tortured by you
My suffering will be ceaseless unless
There where you caressed me
You come again my dearest.

Kibiriti peteroli

Kibiriti, peteroli
Iwapo umeviweka
Hivi ni vitu viwili
Visije kukutanika
Kusalimika muhali
Lazima pataripuka.
Bora ujitenge mbali
Hapo utasalimika.

Katu haiwi salama
Jambo hili ni hakika
Moto kuja ni lazima
Na wala hapana shaka.
Tena tabu kuuzima
Moto ukishanza waka.
Moto vake nina kama
Lazima kuhasirika
Katu usiviamini
Japo kwa dakika
Kabisa havipatani
Mara moja huripuka.
Utangia hatarini
Huwezi kunusurika.
Na jambo hili yakini
Moto hautazimika.

Ahadi

Zilihilifu nyakati
Muhibu ulizosema
Kukawa natafauti

Matches and petrol

Matches and petrol
When you store them
These two things
Must never meet
Nothing would go right
And the whole place would explode
Far better to keep them apart
If peace is to prevail.

No, no peace will prevail
Of that you can be certain
Fire cannot be avoided
Of that you can be sure
Difficult then to quell
When the flames burst into life
Like her too I have a fire
From destruction there's no escape
Trust them at your peril
Never hesitate a second
Utterly incompatible
Primed to spark at once
You have no defense
And there's no one can help you
Of this you can be always sure –
That fire cannot be put out.

The rendezvous

The time you told me
My darling was not correct
I cannot agree that I delayed

Kasorobo saa nzima.
Ulinirudi kwa dhati
Kadiri ya chako kima.

Nalilia kwa laiti
Mahashumu lau kama
Watambua katikati
Huba zangu ni lazima
Ungenionya katiti
Ukafanya na huruma.

Ahadi zina sharuti
Maujudi ni lazima.
Nina hakika mahati
Ya kweli mja husema
Nisamehee wa nguti
Mekosa yangu kalima.

Usiudhike uhuti
Kwa hino yangu kalima
Jumla yako hayati
Kukukosa nimekoma
Najua jaraha mbiti
Haina budi kuuma.

Malaika

Malaika nakupenda Malaika
Naminifanyeje ?
Kijana mwenzio
Nashindua na mali sina, we
Nige kuoa Malaika !

Three quarters of an hour !
But you reproached me sharply
Such is your self-esteem.

Out of remorse I weep
Noble one, how I wish
That you would look inside me
And see how love compels me
Then you'd be gentle in your reproach
And forgive me here and now.

Appointments are sacred things
Of course they must be kept
Of that, esteemed lady, I speak true
The words of your servant ring true
So absolve me, see me kneel before you
My own words were untrue.

Don't be vexed, my sister
By these words I utter
For as long as you live
I'll never let you down
Though a raw wound I know
Is bound to keep on hurting.

Malaika

Malaika, I love you, Malaika
What else can I do ?
I'm as young as you
But I'm unable and I have no wealth
Otherwise I would have married you, Malaika !

Pesa zasimbua roho yangu
Ninge kuoa mama
Ninge kuoa dada
Nashindua na mali sina, we
Ninge kuoa Malaika !

Kidege nakuaza kidege
Ninge kuoa mama
Ninge kuoa dada
Nashindua na mali sina, we
Ninge kuoa Malaika !

TIGRINYA

አስመረት

አንቲ፡ ኩኾብ ዓይና ጽብቔቲ፡ አካይዳ
ጽሐይ፡ ዓራርቦ ምሽት አብ ምውራዳ
ሃሪ ዝመስለ ጸጉራ ወርቂ ክሳዳ
ምሕማቝ ስኢነ ናይ፡ፍቕርኺ0ዳ
አንቲ፡ ኮኾብ ዓይና፡ ጽብቔቲ አካይዳ ።
አስመረት አስመረት
ናይ ሂወት መዋረት
አስመረት ወለላ
ፍቕሪ ዝግብራ ።
መልከ0 ምስ ልቦና ተዓዲላ
ወለላ፡ ናይ ፍቕሪ ዘለላ
ምሳኺ ክነብር ፍቓድኪ አንተኮይኑ
ልበይ፡ የፍስሰልኪ፡ ጥርዓኑ
ዓው ኢለ ክዛረብ፡ ሰሚር ብዘይ ሕፍረት
እወንደ በልኒ አስመረት
እናተጨነቕኩ፡ ክሐስብ ብአኺ

92

Money is the root of all my problems
I would have married you, mama
I would have married you, sister
But I'm unable and I have no wealth
Otherwise I would have married you, Malaika !

Little bird I always think of you, little bird
I would have married you, mama
I would have married you, sister
But I'm unable and I have no wealth
Otherwise I would have married you, Malaika !

TIGRINYA

Asmeret

You whose eyes are like stars
    You walk so beautifully
You're like the rays of the setting sun
    As night is about to fall
Your silken hair and golden neck
    I'm drowning in your love.

Asmeret, Asmeret, life's sweetness
    O Asmeret, sweet as honey.

Enthroned in love you are
    You're as wise as you are beautiful
I'll spend my life with you if you'll let me
    As my heart cries out to you
Without shame I'm on my knees begging you
    Please – tell me that you will, Asmeret.

ሸው ሸው ዝብል ንፋስ
መቻልሕ ድምጽሽ። እናጸዋዕክኒ
ብሽመይ ዓው ኢልኪ
ምስ መቻልሕ መርር መስለኒ ዘሉኺ
አነ። ቄሪጸዮ። ደሪኹኒ። ልበይ።
ሞሳኺ እዮዘሉ ኩሉ ሐሳባተይ
አንወንታ ልብኺ እንተዘይረኺበ
ሂወት። ዋጋ የብላን ምድሪ ምስነሪበ።።
አስመረት አስመረት
ናይ ሂወት መቛረት
አስመረት ወለላ
ፍቕሪ ዝግብራ።።

YORUBA

Ọmọ yin dara o wu wa !

Ọmọ yin dara o wu wa,
Bi egbin l'o ri,
Ọmọ yin dara pupọ,
O nhuwa rere !

Ọmọ wa dara o wu yin,
O s'ọmọ jeje,
Ọmọ wa ki i j'ewuro,
Af'eja dindin !

Iyawo ti a gbe l'anọ,
Bi egbin l'o ri,
Iyawo dara pupọ,
O nhuwa rere !

Asmeret, Asmeret, life's sweetness
      O Asmeret, sweet as honey.

I suffer with my every thought of you
      In the wind I hear your voice call me
I've made up my mind to be with you
      It's my heart's only option.
If you don't give me your answer true
      As the sun sets my life will lose its meaning.

Asmeret, Asmeret, life's sweetness
      O Asmeret, sweet as honey.

—Asghedom W-Michael

YORUBA

Your daughter is beautiful, we love her !

Bridegroom's party: Your daughter is beautiful, we love her !
She is like a gazelle,
She is perfect beauty
She carries herself with such grace !

Bride's party: Our daughter is beautiful, you love her !
She the best of girls
She eats not bitter herbs
But dines on the finest of fish !

Both parties: O yesterday's bride !
She is like a gazelle,
A beautiful bride,
She carries herself with such grace !

Baba mo nlọ o, ye f'adura sin mi

Baba mo nlọ o, ye f'adura sin mi,
Iya mo nlọ o, ye f'adura sin mi,
Ki ng mak'esu ki ng ma k'agbako ni'le ọkọ o,
Baba mo nlọ ọ f'adura sin mi o !

Ẹ ma tori mi o re lọ i jajaku,
Ẹ ma tori mi o re lọ i jajaku,
Ẹni fila mi ba wọ 'ri re l'o maa de o,
Ẹ ma tori mi re lọ i jajaku o !

Agbọkọleri o, e ko ma pantete,
Agbọkọleri o, e ko ma pantete,
B'o ba pantete ategun a gbọkọ lọ o,
Agbọkọleri o ko ma pantete o !

Ọmọ alasọ o, e ko ri gele we,
Ọmọ alasọ o, e ko ri gele we,
E wo gele lori elekurọ gẹnge o,
Ọmọ alasọ ọ ko ri gele we o !

Ifẹ l'akoja ofin o l'aiye o

Ife l'akoja ofin o l'aiye o,
Enia dakun o ẹ lo 'fe !
Ife l'o m'enia meji gbe'nu ile kotopo,
Bi 'fe ko si afin ko le to ẹni meji i gbe.
Ife l'akoja ofin o l'aiye o,
Enia dakun o ẹ lo 'fe !

Ife l'akoja ofin o l'aiye o,

Father, I go to my husband's house

O father, I go to my husband's house, send me with your prayers,
O mother, I go to my husband's house, send me with your prayers,
Let me meet no devil there, let me meet no ill.
Father, I am away, send me with your prayers, oh !

O men, seek not to lay down your lives for my sake,
O men, seek not to lay down your lives for my sake,
Only he whose head my own cap fits will wear it,
O men, seek not to lay down your lives for my sake, oh !

O women, if you carry your man on your head, hold tight,
O women, if you carry your man on your head, hold tight,
Hold him tight left the wind blow him away,
O women, if you carry your man on your head, hold tight, oh !

See the cloth-seller's daughter, her head is bare,
See the cloth-seller's daughter, her head is bare,
See the palmnut-seller's daughter, how gay her head-tie,
See the cloth-seller's daughter, her head is bare, oh !

The fulfilment of this earth's law is love

The fulfilment of this earth's law is love,
So, brothers and sisters, let us practise love !
With love two can live happily in the smallest of rooms
Without love even in a palace two cannot live in peace.
O, the fulfilment of this earth's law is love,
So, brothers and sisters, let us practise love !

The fulfilment of this earth's law is love,

Enia dakun o ẹ lo 'fe !
Ife l'o saju ofin o, o ko o patapata,
Bi 'fẹ ko si irepọ ko le si ninu ajọse.
Ife l'akoja ofin o l'aiye o,
Enia dakun o ẹ lo 'fe !

Ife l'akoja ofin o l'aiye o,
Enia dakun o ẹ lo 'fe !
Ife l'o saju igbeyawo o t'ọkọ t'aya,
Bi 'fẹ ko si ipinya ko le pẹ wọn lati wa ri.
Ife l'akoja ofin o l'aiye o,
Enia dakun o ẹ lo 'fe !

Ife l'akoja ofin o l'aiye o,
Enia dakun o ẹ lo 'fe !
Ife l'o m'enia meji di ọrẹ timọtimọ,
Bi 'fẹ ko si ajaigbula l'awọn ibeji i jẹ.
Ife l'akoja ofin o l'aiye o,
Enia dakun o ẹ lo 'fe !

Ojúmọ́...

Ojúmọ́ t'ó mọ́ mi lóní o
Ojúmọ́ owó ni ó jẹ́...

Ojúmọ́ t'ó mọ́ mi lóní o
Ojúmọ́ ọmọ ni ó jẹ́...

Ojúmọ́ t'ó mọ́ mi lóní o
Ojúmọ́ aya no ó jẹ́...!

So, brothers and sisters, let us practise love !
Love is above the law, and it is the law completely,
Without love there'll be no help of one another.
O, the fulfilment of this earth's law is love,
So, brothers and sisters, let us practise love !

The fulfilment of this earth's law is love,
So, brothers and sisters, let us practise love !
Love comes before marriage of a man and a woman,
Without love cause for separation is not hard to find.
O, the fulfilment of this earth's law is love,
So, brothers and sisters, let us practise love !

The fulfilment of this earth's law is love,
So, brothers and sisters, let us practise love !
With love two may enter the closest friendship,
Without love even twins may be irreconcilable.
O, the fulfilment of this earth's law is love,
So, brothers and sisters, let us practise love !

The day . . .

The day that dawns today
Let it be a day for money . . .

The day that dawns today
Let it be a day for children . . .

The day that dawns today
Let it be a day for wives . . . !

ZULU

Guga mzimba

Guga mzimba sala nhliziyo
Guga sithebe kade wawudlela
Akukho sibonda saguga namagxolo aso
Akukho soka lahlala kahle imbangi ikhala.

Uthando aluboni

Wethu ngilayele laph'eLhona umntahrethu ?
AsiLhona masengimthumbule
Nginjengentandane kulendawo yabu.
Ngidinga nempiko zokundiza
Siphi, hau, siyephi isithandwa sami ?
Ngabe singelapha lento
Phuthumake phela; Into yasendulo:
Uthando aluboni.

Nomakunjenjenje isizungu somntakwethu
Ithemba lihleli kalilahlwa
Kunjengasendulo.
Impindampinda yezinto
Konje nginga shona phina mina ?
Maye ! ngiysphela inbumbulo yakhe
Ngabesingelapha lento
Ngisizeni mpela ngokungilayela
Uthando aluboni.

Siphi hau ! siyephi ?
Isithandwa sami

ZULU

The body perishes

The body perishes, the heart stays young
The platter wears away with serving food
No log retains its bark when old
No lover peaceful while the rival weeps.

Love is blind

Tell me, friend, where is my love ?
When I remember her, I feel an orphan
In this land of ours.
Had I but wings to fly to her –
Where is she, where my love ? –
She would dispel my longing.
Hasten – it is eternal,
Love is blind.

Even while I long for her
Hope is never lost.
It is eternal.
What has gone before shall come again.
Where shall I go ?
O woe ! I die with love of her.
She would dispel my longing.
Help me . . . tell me where she is.
Love is blind.

Where is she,
Where, my love ? –

Ngabe singelapha lento
Hau ! phuthumake phela
Into yasendulo:
Uthando aluboni.

Ngiyoyilobola ngani ?

Ngiyoyilobola ngani ?
Loku inkomo azikho !
Ngoyilobola ngani ?

Ngeke wayithola

Ungibona rigihamba,
Ngizola ngedwa,
Ngikhona, ngisaphila,
Ngeke wayithola !

Imali yami !

Imali yami o, imali yami, yek' imali yami !
Ngamshintsha upondo, ngamenza osheleni !
Ngaqond' eThwathwa, ngaphuza kancane.
Tshelani uSaba o, tshelani umama,
Ngasuk' ekhaya nginesimilo.
Ngafika eGoli ngadliwa izindunduma.
Akenithule zingane zawobaba,
Nginitshele indaba zokuhamba.

She would dispel my longing.
O hasten !
It is eternal,
And love is blind.

With what will I wed her ?

With what will I wed her ?
I possess no cattle !
With what will I wed her ?

You will never get her

So long as you see me walking,
Lost and alone,
So long as I live,
You will never get her !

My money !

My money ! Oh my money !
My money, I am afraid !
I changed a pound to shillings,
I came to the canteen and ate bit by bit.
I changed a pound to shillings,
I came to the canteen and drank bit by bit.
Tell my father, tell my mother.
I am so afraid.

Ngasuk' ekhaya ngiqand' omsebenzi,
Ngafika eGoli ngadliwa ezindunduma.
Ngangimthanda udali umaGumede,
Esitudubeka ududu themba lami.
Ngangimthanda noma ngilambile,
Emafohlefohle ududu themba lami.
Ngangimbanga nempandla engangobaba,
Esitudubeka, ududu themba lami.
Akesihambe siye eThekwini,
Somthola khona umfazi ongcono.

Izibongo

Mafunda-fobele uMthamo unenyembezi
UBhasi Blankie phum' egalaji sikubone,
Sijahe ukugibela siye kwaNongoma.
Yebiya 'zintombi ziyaqoma ziyafika kosala 'kutshelwa onina.

Nansi iNqomanqomane yezintombi.
Ntombi – tom' ubhuti nami ngizoqom' owakho.
Mfula angiphuz' ezakho ngiphuz' i'nduku 'zomile.

I left my home with a good reputation.
I came to Johannesburg and disappeared in the mine dumps.
I loved my dear Magumede,
My darling 'Studebaker', my hope.
I loved her even when I was hungry.
My darling big fat girl, my hope.
My rival was a bald-headed man like my father.
My darling 'Studebaker', my hope.
So let's set off for Durban instead
Where we shall find a better woman.

Praise poem

You gobble up and never chew, swallowing brings tears.
Whitey bus, ride out the garage and let's all see you –
We so want to ride all the way to Nongoma.
All the girls are proposing, and here they come: mothers
        come later to know their own mothers' advice.
See the famous proposer of all the girls.
Girl, love my brother and I'll love yours.
River, I don't drink what's yours – I drink from dry land.

Proverbs of Love

Pato la mahaba, ni haba ni haba.

The gain of love is little, is little.

—*Swahili Proverb*

DAGARI

Sín bɛ́rɛ́ á-yí bá dàng sùùl táá ɛ́.

ŋímɛ́ ní zìl sààn làng kpìɛ̀rɛ̀ tí à má cɛ̀ná táá.

Fʊ̀kʊ̀n tʊ́ɔ́n dé fʊ̀ pɔg-yáá kʊ̀ fʊ̀ dìɛ̀mɛ̀ kà ʊ̀ bàng páár ñíwb zùò fʊ́ ɛ́.

Bà bá dàng bɔ́ pɔ́g kùòr pʊ́ɔ́ ɛ́.

Dɔ́g vìɛ̀lɛ̀ ní zànn vìɛ̀lɛ̀ bá 'ì bwénn é.

Gbílɛ́ bá fúú táá 'à bá kpìɛ̀rɛ̀ bɔ̀g pʊ́ɔ́ ɛ́.

Nʊ́ɔ́n bá dàng cɛ̀ kábír kʊ̀ nʊ́ɔ́n kà ʊ̀ vɔ́l ɛ́.

DARI

Kerì mbaa sa sa mbìtì kɔ̀baná.

Ór si gaarà lòò úrú re.

Gò kuu re úú woo dɔ̀wɔ.

Dùlù te dana díí tè-ni kɔ̀y.

FULFULDE

Tufle mada bana baudo gorum towi naulum.

Debbo goddo dum mama goddo.

Feure te'an amma jo'inta.

To bangado hebai aw'ugo pucu hisa rondugo faggo kam le.

To yide dum nyau, munyal bo dum nyaundigu.

HAUSA

Gwauro ya fi tuzuru ɓarna.

In da abinka a ke ƙamnarka, in babu abinka kare ya fi ka daraja.

Zuma da zaki da harbi.

Nan ke ci nan ke sha mata sun ga rufogon gwabro.

Mai kyau sarki in ba mai kuɗi kusa.

Uwar ɗiya da ɗiya tata duk ka san ba ka gama su aure ba.

Rashin uwa a kan yi uwar ɗaki.

Ba neman aure ke da wuya ba biɗan kuɗi.

Son masoyin wani koshin wahala.

Ba haka aka so ba ƙanen miji ya fi miji kyau.

Proverbs of Love

DAGARI

Two big jars can never lie on top of each other.
Even though the teeth and tongue live together they cut each other.
A son-in-law cannot claim to be a better lover than his father-in-law.
A woman courted at a funeral will leave you at another funeral.
To be born beautiful and to try to be beautiful are not the same thing.
Living together is possible only after many a confrontation.
A bachelor should not woo a woman for another man.

DARI

Too much kindness will kill the feminine sex.
Girls and boys, fire never rests at the side of grass without danger.
Poverty makes you marry a widow.
In wanting to go two ways at once, the sow never starts.

FULFULDE

Hypocrisy is like a woman who carries husband and co-wife on her back.
One man's wife is another man's grandmother.
Lying will get you a wife but not keep her.
If the bride has no horse to ride then spare her carrying the pots and pans.
If love is the sickness then patience is the remedy.

HAUSA

A man no longer married is more dangerous than one not yet married.
If you possess something you will be loved; if you have nothing, even a
    dog will be better respected.
Honey is sweet but it may sting you.
"Let's eat and drink!" said the women on seeing the batchelor's cornbin.
The handsome man is king, if there is no rich man near.
The mother of a daughter and the daughter – you cannot marry both.
Lack of a mother makes one take a wife.
Getting engaged is not hard, paying the money is.
Loving one who loves another is a bellyful of trouble.
The young brother-in-law is preferred to the husband.

In ka ga buduruwar bana da kyau ta baɗi ta fi ta.

Kowa ya bar gida ya bar shi.

Matar na tuba ba ta rasa miji.

Gode Allah wanda ya fi gode uwar matarka, ko da za ta kwace abinta
   Allah ya ba ka wata.

Kishiya mai-ban haushi.

Maso mace wawa bai san za ta ƙi shi ba.

Kekkatta auren so ba abinci.

Ana wahala neman aure ba kuɗi.

Kada a nemi kyau ga matar hamsa kai dai ta yi miya mai zaƙi.

Aure ya tashi, wai an duki bora da ƙaya.

Ba na faye ƙi ba an ce da bazawara ta hau gado.

Jiya ba yau ba tsofuwa ta tuna kwanan gida.

Zamanka kai kaɗai ya fi zama da mugunyar mace.

HAYA

Oburungi bw'omukazi bumanywa iba.

Eishemoi lisindika eitara.

Entare shaija ekasinda eti: lyange, enkazi eti: likwatanisibwe.

Ezisherera tizo ishwera.

Kabikanye afa atashweire.

Murungi timusige enaku zikwita nawe.

Nshweire kubi tahwa bagole.

Nyakahara tagwa mwabo-kula oibone, kagunju oli wambwa.

Engonzi tikushekelana shana ebigilo.

Omukazi atakwendera bawe aba ali mukambuzi weka.

Omukazi mbanzi akugonza mukyagonjanyia.

Owa maka gabili asiba.

Owogonza eiramu tilimugwera.

IGBO

Agboghọ ngaia adi ama mgbe ọ ghara nne di ya.

Nwata rie okeọpka mgahọ ọ hu akatikoro nwanyi, ọ roba ya anya.

Agaghị m eji na enyi m nwanyị mara mma were rịgoo ube e doro iyi.

If you think Miss This-Year is pretty, Miss Next-Year will be more so.
He who deserts his household will be deserted by them.
A woman who admits she is in the wrong won't want for a husband.
Thanking God is better than thanking your mother-in-law: even if she
    takes away her own, God will give to another.
A second wife is a thing of spite.
He who loves a woman is a fool: he never knows if she'll leave him.
A love match without means of support recoils on the makers.
A weary task is trying to marry without money.
Don't seek beauty in a half-dollar wife as long as she makes good soup.
A wife for a man is as certain as his grave.
"I shan't refuse absolutely," said the husbandless woman asked into bed.
Yesterday isn't today, said the old woman remembering nights at home.
Living by yourself is better than living with a bad woman.

HAYA

No man is a hero to his wife.
Two people are better than one.
A respectable home is that of husband and wife.
Love in betrothal never lasts in wedlock.
You get married when you get the partner and not until you get rich.
Being attracted to every beautiful thing will make a man poor.
A man who cannot agree with one woman keeps marrying and divorcing.
A girl has fulfilled her duty when she marries and sticks to her spouse.
The loveliness of a woman is her manners.
A wife who hates her husband's relatives puts strain on her home.
A woman loves her husband while he still loves her.
A polygamist suffers a lot.
The one you love is always wished success.

IGBO

A proud girl knows not when she crosses her mother-in-law.
If you let a young man eat a one-year-old cock, each time he sees a
    succulent woman he'll eye her up.
Just because my girlfriend is beautiful, I won't climb a magic pear tree.

Okokporo na-aba na ụmụaka erighi nne n'ụka, ụmụ ya di ole ?

Nwanyi di ya chọrọ ikpọ asi, adhighi esite ya n'ofe ụtọ.
Onye na-eche enyi ya nwanyi, na-anụ ikiri ukwụ ndi mmụọ.
Nwunye awọ si na di atọka ụtọ, ya jiri nụta nke ya kwọrọ ya n'azụ.

Okeọkpa n'abọ adi anọ n'otu elu ụnọ akwa akwa.
E meghi nwanyi maka nkiri.

KAONDE

Kintojo milemba; mulume kunengela kana wasemapo kana.
Kilembwe walembalala bo blaume, mwenda nabo kesha ukusha pa
    mema.
Ami katete kange umone kunyana yami na kusemena mwana.
Mulume ke Lesa wamumpele.
Buya bwa lupilipili kumona meso.
Pa kivyala po pa bulongo.
Mu kibelo kyashinuka mo muji bantu.
Buko bwaikala ne mu bakabwa.
Kanonyi po basanshila makena ke kabanda kufwa ne.
Kasha katemwa kulakita mushilapya mu lupya wa katataka.
Pa kibangabwe ke bajiminapo bujimi ne.
Nkangalo yo ikosesha nzubo.
Kyaje wa nzolo inge wakokola mwipayai.
Kutemwa buki bwa mayimba kulaba meso.
Lupya lwa kala ke batamo kijiba ne.

LUGANDA

Abaagalana tebafunda.
Akwagala: akuzimbya ku lwazi.
Ayagala omusiiwuufu, y'amunyiriza.
Ekinaawola kikwokeza ki ?
"Kino kiggweeso," nga ne gw'ayagala mw'ajjidde.
Ky'oyagala tekikwagala – gy'okuba olubuto, entumbwe ekubayo
    mabega.

The bachelor who complains that children are few in the Church, how
    many of his children are there ?

A wife whose husband hates her can't save herself by good cooking.

He who waits for his lover hears the footsteps of the spirits.

So sweet was the toad's husband, that ever since her wedding she's
    carried him on her back.

Two cocks will never stay together on one rooftop to crow.

A woman was not made merely for admiration.

KAONDE

A woman cannot be proud of her husband unless he gives her children.

You're too proud: the husband you walk with will leave you in the
    water tomorrow.

Love not only your wife, but her parents too.

My husband was given me by God.

The beauty of pepper is only seen with the eye.

Better to marry a cousin than a stranger.

For a marriage to be good there must be children.

Even dogs have in-laws, so show respect.

A beautiful woman in the area will soon smoke out the adulterers.

Men are attracted to a village where there is a newly arrived woman.

Don't marry someone who is barren.

Husband and wife must be loyal to each other.

If a hen crows, kill it.

If you cheat your wife, sooner or later she'll find out.

If you had one bad marriage in a village, don't go there for another wife.

LUGANDA

Those in love need only the smallest of places.

You'd even build your house on a hard rock for one who loves you.

If you love an ugly person, you make them beautiful.

Why do you let a firebrand burn you if you know it'll eventually cool ?

"No more trouble," you say when the one you love arrives.

A lover who loves you not is like the calf of your leg which turns its
    back on whatever side your stomach turns to.

Kye nkwagala, kiri mu jjinja.

"Leero kino kiggweeso," nga ne gw'oyagala atabadde.

Obutaagalana bukusabisa mukazi wo gonja.

Okwagala, kulya magezi.

Okwambala bulungi si kuwasa bawala, singa akasanke kamaze aba
  wala mu nsi.

Omulungi, ye mwannyina abangi.

Obwavu tebukumanyisa akwagala.

Omulungi aleka emisango, nga tava mu kyalo.

Omulungi alwa, akayuka.

Ow'obusa nnamunnungu, w'atuula w'aleka amaggwa.

"Si musiru, muto," obugole abuyita buganzi.

"Mulungi tansukka," bye biwanga mu nguudo.

Wagumba ennume, n'enduusi we zibeera.

Musisikanye, omuti w'eggye okufumbirwa omunafu.

Eka egwana mukazi ne bba, atalina mukazi azimba ekibanja ?

LUYIA

Amabeyersanio komusimba.

Akhalalyi akhowasio sikhakhumala likhwe khumukongo.

Amakhino amabi sikera iseresi.

Demberesia odekhie.

Kela olole.

Mani komweya ni mwananyina.

Moni tsia mweya tsilangula nitsilutsi.

Namukhasi omukendani auma emiyima.

Nandarakenda yakhwa mungo.

Ndi owetsinyumba tsitsaru oba netsinimi tsitsaru.

Oulalola nyina mulukhana abola baba yafuba emiandu.

MALAGASY

Aza manao fitia ranotrambo: be fihavy fa mora lasa.

Misao-bady tanora ka manome zara ny sasany.

The extent of my love for you is buried in stone.

"No more joy," you say when the one you love goes to war.

When love fades, you have to start asking your wife for your dinner.

Love consumes understanding.

Dressing up does not mean marrying girls – for otherwise the handsome red finch would have snapped up all the girls on earth.

A beautiful woman is the sister of many.

Poverty does not let you know the one who might love you.

A beautiful woman leaves trouble if she won't stop making visits.

Even a beautiful visitor can overstay her welcome.

An unmarried person is like a porcupine: wherever it sits, it leaves spines.

Only someone without experience calls marriage "love."

Boasting "a beautiful woman won't defy me" results in skulls on the road.

Where there are bulls there are also cows.

A cowardly man and a lazy woman are made for each other.

In a home there should be both wife and husband, for does a man with no wife set up a plantation ?

LUYIA

Don't believe in pillow talk.

Another's wife, however pretty, cannot wash your back as your wife can.

Do not be put off by a partner's poor dancing.

Seduce and you will marry.

Marry and see for yourself.

A bride's strength is her kinsfolk.

A bride's eyes pretend not to see.

A woman who moves from husband to husband has no manners.

He who doesn't venture out may marry in his home.

To have three wives you need three tongues.

Only those who never saw their mothers at the height of their beauty say that their fathers have wasted their dowries.

MALAGASY

Let not your love be like a torrent: heavy at first but swiftly abating.

Divorce a young woman and you make another man happy.

Aza manao fitia varavarana, tiana ihany ka atositosika.

Ny fitia toy ny ketsa ka raha afindra dia maniry.
Ny ho vadina betsaka fa ny ho rafozanina no ts'isy.
Tsy ny donak'afo no mahafana ny trano fa ny mpivady mifanaraka.
Vady hariana be tsiny, zanak'olon-tsy vadina toa soa.

MAASAI

Toponie sancha ramatare.

NEMBE

Bará nyanágha buku torú toru.
Iwobó taríbo.
Ma muná toíya, bele darigha.
Sei ére worí wori anga.
Torú kun nina dígha.

OROMO

Calii buutee fi niitii baate nama'tu namaaf deebisa.
Gaarin dhufeef dammi daadhii hin'ta'u.
Gaggaba dhirsa hin'qabu, sagalan heerume jette niitiin.
Haadha ilaalani intala fuudhu.
Heerumni baayeen muratee'rra nama buusa, jette "Niitiin."
Intali haati jaju hiu 'heerumtu.
Jaalalli sardaan jibba sardaa fida.
Karaan ganamaan, fuudhi ijollumman.
Maasii qe'ee fi niitii ganamaa boddee itti galu.
Miidhaga yaadanii, miidhama hiu'yaadan.
Mucaan haadha gaarii qabdu wasiila hin'dhbdu.
Nama mana lamaa yookii qoonqootu ajjeesa, yookii sookootu ajjeesa.
Namni jaalatan gaafa hunkuroo dhufa jette, niitiin.
Niitii dheekkamtu wajjin jiracchu mannaa qofaa jireeennyaa wayya.
Niitiin mari malee fuudhan, mari malee baati.
Rakkataan ulfa fuudha.
Surree fi niitii wajjin kufuu.

Do not treat your loved one like a swinging door: you are fond of it but
   you push it back and forth.

Love is like a young rice-plant: transplant it and it will still grow.

A good wife is easy to find, but suitable in-laws are rare.

The house is not warmed by the fire, but the couple that gets along well.

A man finds many faults in a woman he wants to divorce, and finds
   many charms in a fiancée.

MAASAI

Carry on with your lover as you tend your flock.

NEMBE

A woman you don't have, you can take only with your eyes.

The new one is the loved one.

When cousins fall in love, the pot does not boil.

An ugly wife is abused, but tolerated.

Shy semen won't give birth.

OROMO

Dropped bobbins and recalcitrant wives will be returned to their owner.

Just because your lover has come, honey won't turn into mead.

I have no desire of a husband, said the nine-times married woman.

Observe the mother before marrying the daughter.

Marry too many times and you'll end up with a eunuch.

The girl adored by many will never marry.

Extreme love brings extreme hatred.

To travel is in the morning, to marry is in youth.

To the nearby farm and the wife of one's youth one returns in later life.

To think of beauty and not its dangers is impossible.

The child with a beautiful mother will always have an uncle.

A man with two wives will die of hunger or a curse.

Women say a lover comes while grain is mashing.

Better to live alone than live with an angry wife.

A woman married without her consent runs away without consent.

The poor man marries a pregnant woman.

As trousers fit the man, so a man fits his wife.

SWAHILI

Akipenda chongo huita kengeza.

Barua ya moyo husomwa juu ya panda la uso.

Chozi la akupendaye hutoka kwenye chongo.

Huwezi kurudisha mahaba na maisha.

Kushinda kupendwa, kupenda kushindwa.

Mahaba ni tamu, mahaba ni sumu.

Mapendo kwa asiyekupenda ni sawa mvua porini.

Mapenzi hayana macho, wala hayana maarifa.

Mapenzi ni kikohozi, hayawezi kufichika.

Mapenzi ya kiswibu wawili ndiyo mapenzi.

Mapenzi ya sufuria: hayakawii kupoa.

Moyo hauna subira.

Mwenye kupenda ni jura, wala hana maarifa.

Nyani hutumaini, hupendana mitini.

Pato la mahaba, ni haba ni haba.

Pendo lisilo na kitu, katwa halibainiki.

Si mimi ni moyo.

Songolea si mkuki, kutongoza si kuowa.

Tumekwisha kunywa kahawa, machicha ya mwenye ndoa.

Ukipenda damu upende na usaha.

Wa mtu mtima, u kama kisima.

Aliyeoa binamu hufia vitani.

Dirishani upendo huruka, umaskini uvukapo kizingiti.

Mapenzi ya maskini hayaonekani.

Chanda chema huvikwa pete.

Mlinzi hulinda ndege, mke mzuri halindwi.

Mke ni dada mdogo.

Mke wa kwanza ni kama mama.

Uzuri wa mke ni nguo, wa ng'ombe ni kulimiwa.

Mkeka mpya haulaliwa vema.

Mtu halindi bahari ipitayo kila chombo.

Mume ni moto wa koko, usipowaka utafuka.

Mwenye dada hakosi shemeji.

Proverbs of Love

The one in love calls one-eyed a squint.

A letter from the heart can be read on the face.

The tears of one who loves you will come even from a bad eye.

You cannot bring back love or life.

Victory makes a man popular, to fall in love means to be conquered.

Love is sweet, love is poison.

To give love to one who loves you not is like rain falling on the desert.

Love has neither eyes nor wit.

Love is like a cough, it cannot be hidden.

Love is only love when it affects both sides.

Love is a metal pot: off the fire it cools at once.

The heart has no patience.

He who loves is a fool and has no understanding.

Baboons long to make love in the trees.

The gain of love is little, is little.

Love without gifts does not become evident at all.

It is not I, it is my heart.

A pole is not a spear, seduction is not the same as wedlock.

We've drunk the coffee, the grounds are for your husband.

If you love blood, love pus too.

The heart of a human being is as deep as a well.

He who marries a cousin dies in war.

When poverty crosses the door, love flies out the window.

A poor man's love is never seen.

A handsome finger gets a ring put round it.

A man will shoo birds from the corn, but never a pretty woman.

Your wife is your little sister.

Your first wife is like a mother.

A woman's beauty is her clothing, an ox's is ploughing.

A new sleeping mat is not pleasant to sleep on.

A man does not guard the sea where all the ships pass.

Man is like a jungle fire, if it doesn't burn it'll smoulder.

He who has a sister will not fail to get a brother-in-law.

Ushaufu si heshima ya mwanamke.
Uso mzuri hauhitaji urembo.

TSONGA

I nhonga na xilondza.
Rirhandzu i manghena, hambi ku yiriswile.
A ndzi nyoka leyi dlayaka ntsena, yi tshika; ndzi dlayele ku dya.
Vukati bya katinga.
Hlomisa ri fanele ku sungula hi ku gingirika.
Ku teka kusuhi a ku pfuni.
Mbhuri a xi heti.
U nga twi ku "Xewe": i man' a hlomisa.
Vanhwana mavala ya swimbyanyana, loko swa ha ku hlantiwa.
Munhu un'we a nga kufumeli.
Xikuha nhlovo, van'wana va ta hi ku ka.
Ku teka i ku hoxa nyoka enkwameni.
Murhi wu saseka gon'wo ni marhavi ya wona.
Nuna wa xitekela a rima nsimu yin'we.
X'endza na musi, tshuri ni nkamba u ta swi kuma emahlweni.
Nsati wa ndzhaka a nga na ku sasiwa.
Ayindlu yi xonga hi ku fulelela.
Vuhlalu ringana ni ngoti.
Hi tlhelo dya lirandyu ni mbala, a swi phikisiwi, hikusa mun'wana ni
    mun'wana a randya kumbe a langa swakwe.

TUAREG

Daggel tera a t tumas tafega, umasen as er-sekyaḍ tutela.
Ur é erẓ aw Adem akus wa daɣ isass.

TURKANA

Ebari angaropiyai meere ebari.
Itwaan nipenyintarit alo Turkan ebeyo kane abe ebangana.
Ejok noi akiboikin bon, idwangit akiboi ka aberu nakachalan ori
    makeburan.

An honourable woman never flirts.
A pretty face needs no adornment.

TSONGA

In love like a fly and a wound.
Love is the one who enters someone's heart, even if it is taboo.
I am not a snake which kills its prey and leaves it. I have killed to eat.
Marriage roasts and hardens.
A young wife must work hard at first.
To marry from a family nearby is not good.
A beautiful person will not be perfect.
Ignore many "Good mornings": it's the trick of those anxious to marry.
Eligible girls are like the different colours of newly born puppies.
A person alone does not keep warm.
Digger of the well, others will come only to draw water.
To marry is to put a snake in one's handbag.
A tree is beautiful when its trunk and its branches are beautiful.
A polygamist in love ploughs one field only.
Travel with a pestle and you'll find a mortar and a bowl along your way.
A widow inherited as a wife will never be satisfied.
A house is made beautiful by its thatch.
The beads fit the string exactly.
No one can dispute colours or love: everyone may choose or love as
     they please.

TUAREG

If you think love grows to be a great tree trunk, then bad behaviour
     will be the axe to cut it down.
Man, don't break the vase from which you drink.

TURKANA

Money alone does not make a man rich.
An unmarried person in Turkanaland is called a fool.
It is better to stay alone than with a bad wife.

Ekile lokabanganan ngesi ngolo ereit aberu keng.

Itemokino ekebotonit intari aberu apei, kotere ngaberu nakaalak
    eyaunete ngiogosio.

Aberu naekingaren ngesi ingareni ngaberu nache daana anawi kangina.

Aki dongare arai ayenikin ori nabo erot loiriamunia alone naisaki.

TWI

Ɔba ho yɛ fɛ a, efi ne kunu.

Ɔba na onim kunu.

Ɔbea ne ne kunu asɛm, obi nnim mu.

Mma-dodow kunu yare a, ɔkɔm na ekum no.

Mmea pɛ nea sika wɔ.

Mmea se: wo he yɛ fɛ ! a, ɛne ka.

Obi frɛ wo sɛwose a, mpɛ ntɛm nserew; ebia wo agya yɛ ɔbonnatofo.

Obi mfa osigyafo na n'apɛde nka mu.

Obi mfi bea akyi ntu ne tam.

Obi nkari peredwane nna afa.

Nnamfo banu goru bea bako ho a, ɛnkyɛ na ɔko ba.

Ɔdɔ sene, biribiara ansen bio.

Ɔdɔ nti na nwara fam bo ho.

Ɔdɔ, wonni no sika.

Wo dɔfo kyɛ wo yere a, na wakyɛ wo akasakasa.

Ɔkɔm de hɔho a, ɔda; na odidi me a, obisabisa nkurofo yerenom.

Aware foforo sa ɔde.

Aware rebɔ wo a, wonfwefwɛ mu yɛyere.

Wonkum mmarima a, wɔmfa mmea.

Anosɛmfo biara nnya ɔyere da.

Ninkunu yɛ kɔm a, ɛde mmarima nhina.

Nea ɔrefwefwɛ yere nto mmea ho mpe.

Ɔyere te tɛ kuntu: wode kata wo so a, wo ho keka wo; wuyi gu hɔ nso
    a, awɔw de wo.

Ɔyere nyɛ nam na wɔakyekyɛ amana.

A foolish man is controlled by his wife.

A poor man should only marry one wife, because many wives will cause him much trouble.

The first wife always controls the co-wives in the household.

Dancing is the way to make you famous and to get the girl you desire.

TWI

The beauty of a woman is attributed to her husband.

The pregnant woman alone knows the husband.

Nobody knows the secrets that exist between a husband and a wife.

When a man who has many wives is sick, he dies of starvation.

Women like to be where there is money.

If women say you are handsome, it means you are soon to incur debts.

If someone says you are the very image of your father, do not laugh too quickly – perhaps your father is a womanizer.

No one goes to bed with an unmarried woman without giving her something.

No one can take the loincloth off a woman without her knowledge.

Nobody pays a dowry of 36 dollars and then sleeps alone.

If two friends flirt with one woman, a fight will soon ensue.

Love is the greatest of all virtues.

It's love that makes the seashell stick to the rock.

Love is not based on wealth.

If your good friend gives you a wife, he gives you a quarrel.

When a stranger hungers, he sleeps; but when he's full he asks about other people's wives.

A new marriage picks out the good yam.

If a couple wish to divorce, they don't look deeply for a reason.

If you don't kill the men, you can't take their women.

People who boast will never find a wife.

If jealousy caused hunger, then all men would be hungry.

He who seeks a wife doesn't speak ill of women.

A wife is like a woolen blanket: if you cover yourself with it, you itch; if you take it away, you feel cold.

A wife is not meant to be sent to someone else as a gift.

Ayere-dodow yɛ ohia na ɛnyɛ five.
Ɔye-pa sen sika.
Wo yerenom anum a, wɔ tɛkrɛma anum.

WOLOF

Jabar, doonte ne yeena jélloy sàkket, ab xer damm.
Bëggum ñeex duma taxa dëppoo cin lu tàng.
Benn loxo du tàccu.
Bu la taar bi taxa lew, ndax laago du wees.
Bëtub mbëggeel jéll nab gàkk.

YAKA

Mwaana nkheeto kakodi, tsuku aandi yakala: mwaana yakala kakodi,
    tsuku aandi nkheeto.
Kitsia ntima, bayakala mu kwiisa bena.
Nkheeto khoombo, yakala kaasu di baanga.
Nkheeto kamoni mbvula, yakala kamoni sanga-nguungu.
Nkheeto mosi kaloondo tsaambu.
Bakhoomgo batatu, ngyungani kakoondaako.

Loongo lwa mbisi: nkheeto ku thaandu, yakala ku baanda.
Ki diidi nkheeto, ki diidi yakala; ki diidi yakala, ki diidi nkheeto.
Khoko wakola mbvula ku m-mbeemba, nkheeto tya yakala ku
    yimoko.
Mbuundu zowa wanyeenga nkasi ngani kakoonda kweela.

YORUBA

Òjò pa mi, òjò kpa ewa ara mi danu.
Etutu ko fẹ pòròpóó de inu: kinun l'ọ mọ-araiye ifẹ 'ni mọ.

Òjò ni oko agbado.
Eni fe arewa fe iyọ nu.
À kì í dóko dí gbèsè; omọ la fi mbí.
A kì í ko elésin ká wá lọ fé elésè.
A kì í mọ oko ká tún mọ àlèe rè.

Too many wives cause poverty, but it doesn't matter.
A good wife is more precious than gold.
If you have five wives, you have five different tongues.

WOLOF

A wife is like a garden fence: there's always a broken post.
Just because I want sauce, I won't tip the hot pot over my head.
A lone hand does not applaud.
Don't be too proud of your beauty, a sickness can always arrive.
The look of love slices through all faults.

YAKA

As a girl grows up, her goal is a husband; as a boy grows, his is a
  wife.
Soothe your heart, there are plenty more young men in the world.
Woman is like the goat, man is like the red kola nut.
Woman sees rain, while man sees spiders.
A single woman is like a jug in a basket.
If a man has three wives, one will roam like an orphan, another when
  sent for will refuse.
The marriage of animals: the female upstream, the male downstream.
What a woman eats, a man eats too; what a man eats, so will a woman.
A cock chases the rain with its tail, a woman shows her love towards
  her husband in small-talk.
The heart is mad: it falls in love with one who is another's.

YORUBA

It rains down on me but the drops cannot wash away my beauty.
White ants do not really love the dry stalk of corn: those we think
  love us, love us only a little.
Rain is the husband of maize.
He who marries beauty marries trouble.
One does not marry to get into debt, one marries to get children.
You don't divorce a horse-rider and then marry a pedestrian.
Don't recognise your daughter's suitor yet welcome her lover on the side.

A kì í tú ọmọge láṣọ tan ká tún máa wò ó lójú.

Aya òlẹ là ngbà; a kì í gba ọmọ òlẹ.

Bí a bá fi owó kan fi ọmọ fún ọkọ, owó méwàá kì í ṣeé gbà á mọ́.

Bí a kò bá lè mú ọkọlóbìnrin, a kì í na obìnrin rẹ̀.

Bí obìnrin kò bá gbé ilé ọkọ méjì, kì í mọ èyí tó sàn.

Eni ti a bá mmú ìyàwó bò wá fún kì í garùn.

Ẹni tó gba ọnà ẹbùrú wá ta ojì: wọ́n ní a kì í gba ọnà ẹbùrú wá ta ojì; ó ní ṣé a lè gba ọnà ojúlé ? Wọ́n ní bẹ̀ẹ̀ ni.

Ohun méta ni a kì í wí pé kí òré ẹni má ṣe: a kì í wí pé kí òré ẹni má kòólẹ́; a kì í wí pé kí òré ẹni má nìí obìnrin; a kì í wí pé kí òré ẹni má lo sí ìdálẹ̀.

Ojú kì í pọ́nni ká fi àbúrò ẹni ṣaya.

Oju kì í ri arẹwà kó má kìí i.

Ojú kì í ti ọkọ kó má bàá ìyàwóo rẹ̀ sòrò.

Ọba kì í kọ obìnrin sílẹ̀ tán kí tálákà lọ fẹ́ ẹ sílé.

Etutu ko fẹ pòròpóró de inu, kinun l'ọmọ-araiye ife 'ni mọ.

Òjò ni ọkọ agbado.

Eni fe arewa fẹ iyọnu.

Ẹni ti o ni ẹwà ko ni ẹwa, ẹni ti o l'ẹwa, ko l'ẹwà.

ZULU

Umendo kawuthunyelwa gundane.

Umendo kawubhulelwa.

Ukwenda wukuzilahla.

Uthand' alukheti ludwan' oluwela kulona.

Zal' abantu ziy' ebantwinni; akuntomb' iyogan' inyamazane.

Induku kayinamuzi.

Intomb' ayiluthez' olumanzi.

Isoka aliganwa; kuganwa intolela mlonyeni.

Amasongo akhala emabili.

One does not undress a maiden and then sit gazing into her eyes.

Take an unlucky man's wife, but leave his child.

If you marry off a girl with one hand, ten hands will not bring her back.

If you are no match for a woman's husband, don't hit her instead.

A woman who has not lived with two husbands will never know which is the better.

He to whom a bride is being brought does not stretch his neck.

The man who came by the back door to complain about a cuckolder was told to come through the front door.

Three things you cannot forbid your friend from doing: building a house, getting married and starting a journey.

One is never so desperate as to make one's sister one's wife.

Eyes never see a beautiful woman without greeting her.

A husband is never too shy that he can't speak to his wife.

A king will not divorce a woman only for a poverty-stricken man to marry her.

White ants don't really love their cornstalk; those we think love us, love us only a little.

Rain is the husband of maize.

He who marries beauty marries trouble.

One who has beauty has no wealth; one who has wealth has no beauty.

ZULU

No mouse is sent when one is to marry.

Marriage is not divined for.

To marry is to throw oneself away.

Love does not choose the blade of grass on which it falls.

Women reject men but go to men; for no woman will ever marry a wild beast.

A stick has no household.

A maiden does not collect wet fuel.

A young man popular with the girls doesn't marry; old men do.

Rings make a sound if there are two.

AFRICA

BERBER

COPTIC
EGYPTIAN
ANCIENT
EGYPTIAN

TUAREG

DAGARI

FULFULDE
KRIO   HAUSA   DARI
MANDINKA
WOLOF YORUBA
TWI   IGBO
NEMBE

TIGRINYA
AMHARIC
AFAR
OROMO
LUGANDA SOMALI
TURKANA
MBOSI   LUYIA
MAASAI
YAKA   SWAHILI

HAYA
KAONDE
LALA
BEMBA
SHONA   MALAGA
TSONGA
SESOTHO
ZULU